Weather and Climate Inventory
National Park Service
Upper Columbia Basin Network

Natural Resource Technical Report NPS/UCBN/NRTR—2006/012
WRCC Report 2006-11

Christopher A. Davey, Kelly T. Redmond, and David B. Simeral
Western Regional Climate Center
Desert Research Institute
2215 Raggio Parkway
Reno, Nevada 89512-1095

November 2006

U.S. Department of the Interior
National Park Service
Natural Resource Program Center
Fort Collins, Colorado

The Natural Resource Publication series addresses natural resource topics that are of interest and applicability to a broad readership in the National Park Service and to others in the management of natural resources, including the scientific community, the public, and the National Park Service conservation and environmental constituencies. Manuscripts are peer-reviewed to ensure that the information is scientifically credible, technically accurate, appropriately written for the intended audience, and designed and published in a professional manner.

The Natural Resources Technical Reports series is used to disseminate the peer-reviewed results of scientific studies in the physical, biological, and social sciences for both the advancement of science and the achievement of the National Park Service mission. The reports provide contributors with a forum for displaying comprehensive data that are often deleted from journals because of page limitations. Current examples of such reports include the results of research that address natural resource management issues; natural resource inventory and monitoring activities; resource assessment reports; scientific literature reviews; and peer-reviewed proceedings of technical workshops, conferences, or symposia.

Views and conclusions in this report are those of the authors and do not necessarily reflect policies of the National Park Service. Mention of trade names or commercial products does not constitute endorsement or recommendation for use by the National Park Service.

Printed copies of reports in these series may be produced in a limited quantity and they are only available as long as the supply lasts. This report is also available from the Natural Resource Publications Management website (http://www.nature.nps.gov/publications/NRPM) on the Internet or by sending a request to the address on the back cover.

Please cite this publication as follows:

Davey, C. A., K. T. Redmond, and D. B. Simeral. 2006. Weather and Climate Inventory, National Park Service, Upper Columbia Basin Network. Natural Resource Technical Report NPS/UCBN/NRTR—2006/012. National Park Service, Fort Collins, Colorado.

NPS/UCBN/NRTR—2006/012, November 2006

Contents

Figures

Tables

Appendixes

Acronyms

AASC	American Association of State Climatologists
ACIS	Applied Climate Information System
AgriMet	Pacific Northwest Cooperative Agricultural Network
ARL FRD	NOAA Air Resources Laboratory Field Research Division
ASOS	Automated Surface Observing System
AWOS	Automated Weather Observing System
BIHO	Big Hole National Battlefield
BLM	Bureau of Land Management
CANADA	Canadian weather/climate stations
CASTNet	Clean Air Status and Trends Network
CIRO	City of Rocks National Reserve
COOP	NWS Cooperative Observer Program
CRMO	Craters of the Moon National Monument and Preserve
CRN	Climate Reference Network
CWOP	Citizen Weather Observer Program
DFIR	Double-Fence Intercomparison Reference
DST	daylight savings time
ENSO	El Niño Southern Oscillation
EPA	Environmental Protection Agency
FAA	Federal Aviation Administration
FIPS	Federal Information Processing Standards
GMT	Greenwich Mean Time
GPMP	NPS Gaseous Pollutant Monitoring Program
GOES	Geostationary Operational Environmental Satellite
GPS	Global Positioning System
HAFO	Hagerman Fossil Beds National Monument
I&M	NPS Inventory and Monitoring Program
ITD	Idaho Transportation Department network
JODA	John Day Fossil Beds National Monument
KBCI	KBCI TV, Boise, Idaho
LARO	Lake Roosevelt National Recreation Area
LST	local standard time
MCSCN	Montana Counties Soil Climate Network
MIIN	Minidoka Internment National Monument
MSOWFO	NWS Forecast Office, Missoula, Montana
NADP	National Atmospheric Deposition Program
NCDC	National Climatic Data Center
NEPE	Nez Perce National Historical Park
NetCDF	Network Common Data Form
NOAA	National Oceanic and Atmospheric Administration
NPS	National Park Service
NRCS	Natural Resources Conservation Service
NRCS-SC	NRCS snowcourse network
NWS	National Weather Service

ODOT	Oregon Department of Transportation network
PDO	Pacific Decadal Oscillation
PDTWFO	NWS Forecast Office, Pendleton, Oregon
PNA	Pacific-North America Oscillation
PRISM	Parameter Regression on Independent Slopes Model
RAWS	Remote Automated Weather Station network
RCC	regional climate center
SAO	NWS/FAA Surface Airways Observation network
SOD	Summary Of the Day
Surfrad	Surface Radiation Budget network
SNOTEL	NRCS Snowfall Telemetry network
UCBN	Upper Columbia Basin Inventory and Monitoring Network
UPR	Union Pacific Railroad network
USDA	U.S. Department of Agriculture
USGCRP	U.S. Global Change Research Program
USGS	U.S. Geological Survey
UTC	Coordinated Universal Time
WA DOT	Washington State Department of Transportation network
WBAN	Weather Bureau Army Navy
WHMI	Whitman Mission National Historic Site
WRCC	Western Regional Climate Center
WMO	World Meteorological Organization

Executive Summary

Climate is a dominant factor driving the physical and ecologic processes affecting the Upper Columbia Basin Inventory and Monitoring Network (UCBN). Climate variations are responsible for short- and long-term changes in ecosystem fluxes of energy and matter and have profound effects on underlying geomorphic and biogeochemical processes. Historic glaciation events have had a tremendous effect on modern day geomorphology as well as land use practices in the UCBN. Projected climate changes in the UCBN could increase fire frequency and intensity, as well as the invasion rates of exotic plant and pest species. Because of its influence on the ecology of UCBN park units and the surrounding areas, climate was identified as a high-priority vital sign for UCBN, and climate is one of the 12 basic inventories to be completed for all National Park Service (NPS) Inventory and Monitoring Program (I&M) networks.

This project was initiated to inventory past and present climate monitoring efforts. In this report, we provide the following information:

- Overview of broad-scale climatic factors and zones important to UCBN park units.
- Inventory of weather and climate station locations in and near UCBN park units relevant to the NPS I&M Program.
- Results of an inventory of metadata on each weather station, including affiliations for weather-monitoring networks, types of measurements recorded at these stations, and information about the actual measurements (length of record, etc.).
- Initial evaluation of the adequacy of coverage for existing weather stations and recommendations for improvements in monitoring weather and climate.

The UCBN is in a transitional semi-arid climate zone and, being located generally between the Cascades and the Rocky Mountains, its climate patterns are dominated by topographic features. Mean annual precipitation in the UCBN ranges from just under 250 mm near Hagerman Fossil Beds National Monument (HAFO) to 750 mm or greater near Big Hole National Battlefield (BIHO) and some of the units of Nez Perce National Historical Park (NEPE). Most of this precipitation accumulates during the winter, especially in western portions of the UCBN. Eastern portions of the UCBN, however, can obtain much of their annual precipitation during the spring and summer months. Temperatures in the UCBN are influenced primarily by elevation, with mean annual temperatures reaching 10°C for lower-elevation park units such as Whitman Mission National Historic Site (WHMI) and dropping as low as 1°C for BIHO and other high-mountain valleys. An east-west gradient is evident in winter and mean annual temperatures as the eastern portion of the UCBN is influenced more strongly by cold continental and polar air masses moving southward from Canada during the winter months. Winter temperatures in the eastern part of the UCBN have been as low as -48°C. The warmest summer locations in the UCBN are those park units located in the lower portions of the Snake River Plain, such as HAFO. July maximum temperatures in these areas reach 30°C commonly and sometimes can exceed 45°C. The Pacific-North America Oscillation (PNA) influences storm frequency in the UCBN during a given year. Both the El Niño Southern Oscillation (ENSO) and the Pacific Decadal Oscillation (PDO) cause interannual climate variations in the UCBN. Precipitation time series in the UCBN do not show a significant trend but temperature time series do clearly show warming.

Through a search of national databases and inquiries to NPS staff, we have identified 14 weather and climate stations within UCBN park units. These include five stations in Craters of the Moon National Monument and Preserve (CRMO), five stations in Lake Roosevelt National Recreation Area (LARO), two stations in John Day Fossil Beds National Monument (JODA), and one station each in Nez Perce National Historical Park (NEPE) and Whitman Mission National Historic Site (WHMI). Metadata and data records for most of the weather and climate stations identified for UCBN are sufficiently complete and satisfactory in quality.

A few of the UCBN park units have satisfactory coverage of weather and climate stations, including the availability of both long-term climate records and near-real-time weather data either in or near the park units. These park units include HAFO, LARO, Minidoka Internment National Monument (MIIN), NEPE, and WHMI.

Other park units that currently have no weather or climate stations could benefit from the installation of additional stations. The availability of near-real-time weather data is limited for BIHO. The closest representative automated station is almost 40 km northeast of the park unit. The NPS might consider either installing an automated station at BIHO, such as a Remote Automated Weather Station (RAWS), or working with the Natural Resources Conservation Service (NRCS) to upgrade the existing snowcourse site at Gibbons Pass to a Snowfall Telemetry Network (SNOTEL) station. This would provide much-needed near-real-time data in the Big Hole Valley that could be used in various environmental studies.

Almost all of the weather/climate stations we identified for City of Rocks National Reserve (CIRO) are located in the lower-elevation basins surrounding the Albion Mountains and are therefore less representative of CIRO, located in the Albion Mountains. All of the stations identified for CIRO are at least 30 km from CIRO. Due to the very limited station coverage around CIRO, there are no manual or automated stations within 30 km of CIRO. An additional automated station in the region would greatly improve weather monitoring efforts for CIRO. One possibility would be to upgrade the snowcourse station "Boy Scout Camp" to a SNOTEL station.

The COOP stations presently within JODA units have data records that are of questionable quality. In particular, the COOP station "Dayville 8 NW" regularly lacks weekend observations. Taking efforts to ensure weekend observations are made at this station will benefit NPS. Installing an automated station such as a RAWS station at one of the JODA units may also be feasible, since there are generally no automated stations within 20 km of any of the JODA units.

Almost all of the weather/climate stations identified within CRMO are located at or near the main visitor center, in the northern part of the park unit. Stations are lacking throughout the southern half of CRMO. NPS could therefore benefit by teaming up with either RAWS agencies or the National Oceanic and Atmospheric Administration Air Resources Laboratory Field Research Division network (ARL FRD) to install an automated station in the southern half of CRMO. These are the primary automated networks in the vicinity of CRMO. While a RAWS station is less costly, technical assistance and maintenance is more readily available for ARL FRD stations in the area.

Acknowledgements

This work was supported and completed under Task Agreement H8R07010001, with the Great Basin Cooperative Ecosystem Studies Unit. We would like to acknowledge very helpful assistance from various National Park Service personnel associated with the Upper Columbia Basin Inventory and Monitoring Network. Particular thanks are extended to Lisa Garrett. We also thank John Gross, Margaret Beer, Grant Kelly, Greg McCurdy, and Heather Angeloff for all their help. Portions of the work were supported by the NOAA Western Regional Climate Center.

1.0. Introduction

Weather and climate are key drivers in ecosystem structure and function. Global- and regional-scale climate variations will have a tremendous impact on natural systems (Chapin et al. 1996; Schlesinger 1997; Jacobson et al. 2000; Bonan 2002). Long-term patterns in temperature and precipitation provide first-order constraints on potential ecosystem structure and function. Secondary constraints are realized from the intensity and duration of individual weather events and, additionally, from seasonality and inter-annual climate variability. These constraints influence the fundamental properties of ecologic systems, such as soil–water relationships, plant–soil processes, and nutrient cycling, as well as disturbance rates and intensity. These properties, in turn, influence the life-history strategies supported by a climatic regime (Neilson 1987; Garrett et al. 2005).

Given the importance of climate, it is one of 12 basic inventories to be completed by the National Park Service (NPS) Inventory and Monitoring Program (I&M) network (I&M 2006). As primary environmental drivers for the other vital signs, weather and climate patterns present various practical and management consequences and implications for the NPS (Oakley et al. 2003). Most park units observe weather and climate elements as part of their overall mission. The lands under NPS stewardship provide many excellent locations for monitoring climatic conditions.

It is essential that park units within the Upper Columbia Basin Inventory and Monitoring Network (UCBN) have an effective climate-monitoring system in place to track climate changes and to aid in management decisions relating to these changes. The purpose of this report is to determine the current status of weather and climate monitoring within UCBN (Figure 1.1; Table 1.1). In this report, we provide the following informational elements:

- Overview of broad-scale climatic factors and zones important to UCBN park units.
- Inventory of locations for all weather stations in and near UCBN park units that are relevant to the NPS I&M networks.
- Results of metadata inventory for each station, including weather-monitoring network affiliations, types of recorded measurements, and information about actual measurements (length of record, etc.).
- Initial evaluation of the adequacy of coverage for existing weather stations and recommendations for improvements in monitoring weather and climate.

1.1. Network Terminology

Before proceeding, it is important to stress that this report discusses the idea of "networks" in two different ways. Modifiers are used to distinguish between NPS I&M networks and weather/climate station networks. See Appendix B for a full definition of these terms.

1.1.1. Weather/Climate Station Networks

Most weather and climate measurements are made not from isolated stations but from stations that are part of a network operated in support of a particular mission. The limiting case is a network of one station, where measurements are made by an interested observer or group. Larger networks usually have more and better inventory data and station-tracking procedures. Some national weather/climate networks are associated with the National Oceanic and Atmospheric

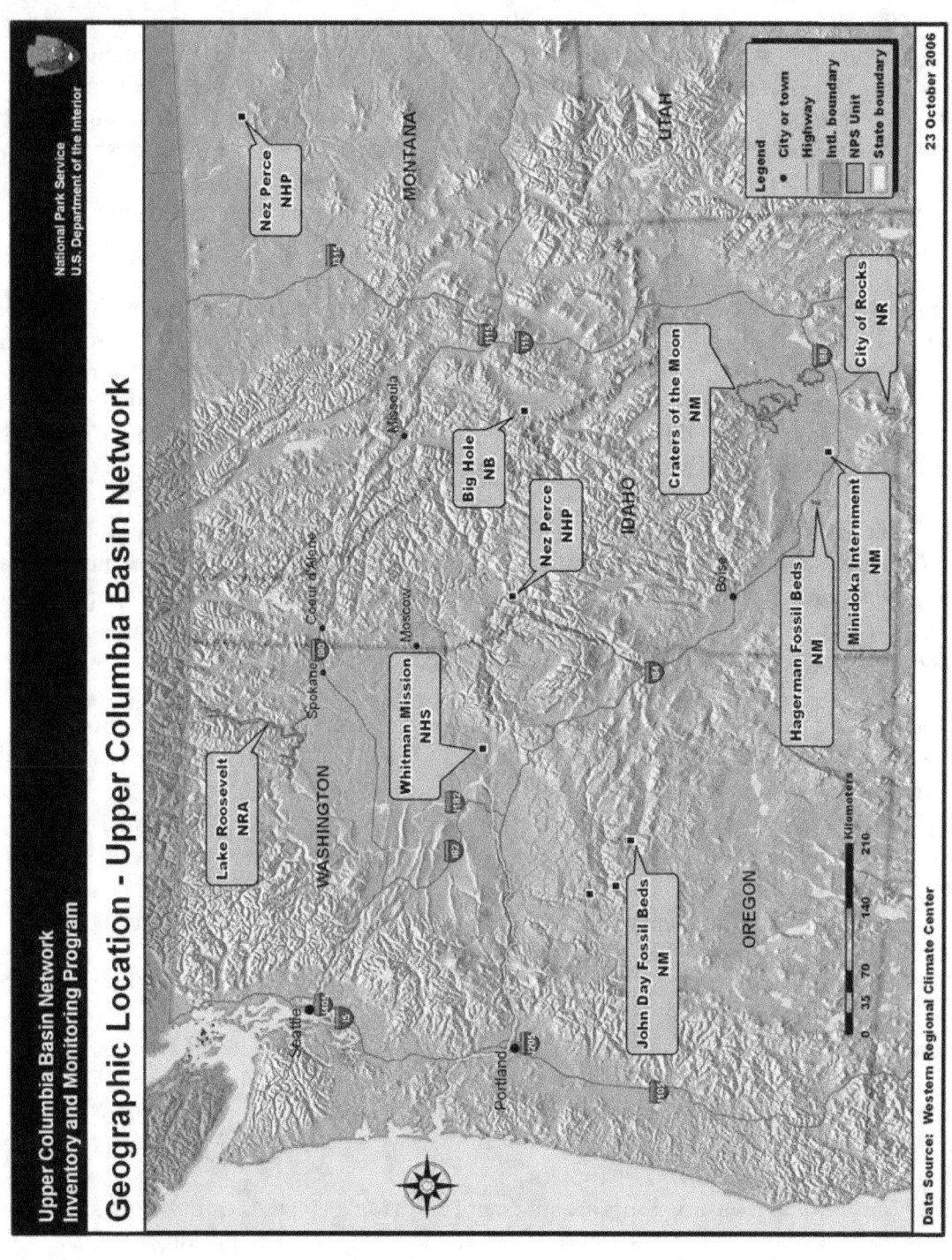

Figure 1.1. Map of the Upper Columbia Basin Network.

Table 1.1. Park units in the UCBN.

Acronym	Name
BIHO	Big Hole National Battlefield
CIRO	City of Rocks National Reserve
CRMO	Craters of the Moon National Monument and Preserve
HAFO	Hagerman Fossil Beds National Monument
JODA	John Day Fossil Beds National Monument
LARO	Lake Roosevelt National Recreation Area
MIIN	Minidoka Internment National Monument
NEPE	Nez Perce National Historical Park
WHMI	Whitman Mission National Historic Site

Administration (NOAA), including the National Weather Service (NWS) Cooperative Observer Program (COOP). Other national networks include the interagency Remote Automated Weather Station network (RAWS) and the U.S. Department of Agriculture/Natural Resources Conservation Service (USDA/NRCS) Snowfall Telemetry (SNOTEL) and snowcourse networks. Usually a single agency, but sometimes a consortium of interested parties, will jointly support a particular weather/climate network.

1.1.2. NPS I&M Networks
Within the NPS, the system for monitoring various attributes in the participating park units (about 270–280 in total) is divided into 32 NPS I&M networks. These networks are collections of park units grouped together around a common theme, typically geographical.

1.2. Weather versus Climate Definitions
It is also important to distinguish whether the primary use of a given station is for weather purposes or for climate purposes. Weather station networks are intended for near-real-time usage, where the precise circumstances of a set of measurements are typically less important. In these cases, changes in exposure or other attributes over time are not as critical. Climate networks, however, are intended for long-term tracking of atmospheric conditions. Siting and exposure are critical factors for climate networks, and it is vitally important that the observational circumstances remain essentially unchanged over the duration of the station record. Some climate networks can be considered hybrids of weather/climate networks. These hybrid climate networks can supply information on a short-term "weather" time scale and a longer-term "climate" time scale.

In this report, "weather" generally refers to current (or near-real-time) atmospheric conditions, while "climate" is defined as the complete ensemble of statistical descriptors for temporal and spatial properties of atmospheric behavior (see Appendix B). Climate and weather phenomena shade gradually into each other and are ultimately inseparable.

1.3. Purpose of Measurement

Climate inventory and monitoring climate activities should be based on a set of guiding fundamental principles. Any evaluation of weather/climate monitoring programs begins with asking the following question:

- What is the purpose of weather and climate measurements?

Evaluation of past, present, or planned weather/climate monitoring activities must be based on the answer to this question.

Weather and climate data and information constitute a prominent and widely-requested component of the NPS I&M networks (I&M 2006). Within the context of the NPS, the following services constitute the main purposes for recording weather and climate observations:

- Provide measurements for real-time operational needs and early warnings of potential hazards (landslides, mudflows, washouts, fallen trees, plowing activities, fire conditions, aircraft and watercraft conditions, road conditions, rescue conditions, fog, restoration and remediation activities, etc.).
- Provide visitor education and aid interpretation of expected and actual conditions for visitors while they are in the park and for deciding if and when to visit the park.
- Establish engineering and design criteria for structures, roads, culverts, etc., for human comfort, safety, and economic needs.
- Consistently monitor climate over the long-term to detect changes in environmental drivers affecting ecosystems, including both gradual and sudden events.
- Provide retrospective data to understand *a posteriori* changes in flora and fauna.
- Document for posterity the physical conditions in and near the park units, including mean, extreme, and variable measurements (in time and space) for all applications.

The last three items in the preceding list are pertinent primarily to the NPS I&M networks; however, all items are important to NPS operations and management. Most of the needs in this list overlap heavily. It is often impractical to operate separate climate measuring systems that also cannot be used to meet ordinary weather needs, where there is greater emphasis on timeliness and reliability.

1.4. Design of Climate-Monitoring Programs

Determining the purposes for collecting measurements in a given weather/climate monitoring program will guide the process of identifying weather/climate stations suitable for the monitoring program. The context for making these decisions is provided in Chapter 2, where background on the UCBN climate is presented. However, this process is only one step in evaluating and designing a climate-monitoring program. This process includes the following additional steps:

- Define park and network-specific monitoring needs and objectives.
- Identify locations and data repositories of existing and historic stations.
- Acquire existing data when necessary or practical.
- Evaluate the quality of existing data.
- Evaluate the adequacy of coverage of existing stations.

- Develop a protocol for monitoring the weather and climate, including the following:
  - o Standardized summaries and reports of weather/climate data.
  - o Data management (quality assurance and quality control, archiving, data access, etc.).
- Develop and implement a plan for installing or modifying stations, as necessary.

Throughout the design process, there are various factors that require consideration in evaluating weather and climate measurements. Many of these factors have been summarized by Dr. Tom Karl, director of the NOAA National Climatic Data Center (NCDC), and widely distributed as the "Ten Principles for Climate Monitoring" (Karl et al. 1996; NRC 2001). These principals are presented in Appendix A, and the guidelines are embodied in many of the comments made throughout this report. The most critical factors are presented here. In addition, an overview of requirements necessary to operate a climate network is provided in Appendix C, with further discussion in Appendix E.

1.4.1. Need for Consistency

A principal goal in climate monitoring is to detect and characterize slow and sudden changes in climate through time. This is of less concern for day-to-day weather changes, but it is of paramount importance for climate variability and change. There are many ways whereby changes in techniques for making measurements, changes in instruments or their exposures, or seemingly innocuous changes in site characteristics can lead to apparent changes in climate. Safeguards must be in place to avoid these false sources of temporal "climate" variability if we are to draw correct inferences about climate behavior over time from archived measurements.

For climate monitoring, consistency through time is vital, counting at least as important as absolute accuracy. Sensors record only what is occurring at the sensor—this is all they can detect. It is the responsibility of station or station network managers to ensure that observations are representative of the spatial and temporal climate scales that we wish to record.

1.4.2. Metadata

Changes in instruments, site characteristics, and observing methodologies can lead to apparent changes in climate through time. It is therefore vital to document all factors that can bear on the interpretation of climate measurements and to update the information repeatedly through time. This information ("metadata," data about data) has its own history and set of quality-control issues that parallel those of the actual data. There is no single standard for the content of climate metadata, but a simple rule suffices:

- Observers should record all information that could be needed in the future to interpret observations correctly without benefit of the observers' personal recollections.

Such documentation includes notes, drawings, site forms, and photos, which can be of inestimable value if taken in the correct manner. That stated, it is not always clear to the metadata provider *what is important* for posterity and *what will be important* in the future. It is almost impossible to "over document" a station. Station documentation is greatly underappreciated and is seldom thorough enough (especially for climate purposes). Insufficient attention to this issue often lowers the present and especially future value of otherwise useful data.

The convention followed throughout climatology is to refer to metadata as information about the measurement process, station circumstances, and data. The term "data" is reserved solely for the actual weather and climate records obtained from sensors.

1.4.3. Maintenance

Inattention to maintenance is the greatest source of failure in weather/climate stations and networks. Problems begin to occur soon after sites are deployed. A regular visit schedule must be implemented, where sites, settings (e.g., vegetation), sensors, communications, and data flow are checked routinely (once or twice a year at a minimum) and updated as necessary. Parts must be changed out for periodic recalibration or replacement. With adequate maintenance, the entire instrument suite should be replaced or completely refurbished about once every five to seven years.

Simple preventative maintenance is effective but requires much planning and skilled technical staff. Changes in technology and products require retraining and continual re-education. Travel, logistics, scheduling, and seasonal access restrictions consume major amounts of time and budget but are absolutely necessary. Without such attention, data gradually become less credible and then often are misused or not used at all.

1.4.4. Automated versus Manual Stations

Historic stations often have depended on manual observations and many continue to operate in this mode. Manual observations frequently produce excellent data sets. Sensors and data are simple and intuitive, well tested, and relatively cheap. Manual stations have much to offer in certain circumstances and can be a source of both primary and backup data. However, methodical consistency for manual measurements is a constant challenge, especially with a mobile work force. Operating manual stations takes time and needs to be done on a regular schedule, though sometimes the routine is welcome.

Nearly all newer stations are automated. Automated stations provide better time resolution, increased (though imperfect) reliability, greater capacity for data storage, and improved accessibility to large amounts of data. The purchase cost for automated stations is higher than for manual stations. A common expectation and serious misconception is that an automated station can be deployed and left to operate on its own. In reality, automation does not eliminate the need for people but rather changes the type of person that is needed. Skilled technical personnel are needed and must be readily available, especially if live communications exist and data gaps are not wanted. Site visits are needed at least annually and spare parts must be maintained. Typical annual costs for sensors and maintenance are $1500–2500 per station per year.

1.4.5. Communications

With manual stations, the observer is responsible for recording and transmitting station data. Data from automated stations, however, can be transmitted quickly for access by research and operations personnel, which is a highly preferable situation. A comparison of communication systems for automated and manual stations shows that automated stations generally require additional equipment, more power, higher transmission costs, attention to sources of disruption or garbling, and backup procedures (e.g. manual downloads from data loggers).

Automated stations are capable of functioning normally without communication and retaining many months of data. At such sites, however, alerts about station problems are not possible, large gaps can accrue when accessible stations quit, and the constituencies needed to support such stations are smaller and less vocal. Two-way communications permit full recovery from disruptions, ability to reprogram data loggers remotely, and better opportunities for diagnostics and troubleshooting. In virtually all cases, two-way communications are much preferred to all other communication methods. However, two-way communications require considerations of cost, signal access, transmission rates, interference, and methods for keeping sensor and communication power loops separate. Two-way communications are frequently impossible (no service) or impractical, expensive, or power consumptive. Two-way methods (cellular, land line, radio, Internet) require smaller up-front costs as compared to other methods of communication and have variable recurrent costs, starting at zero. Satellite links work everywhere (except when blocked by trees or cliffs) and are quite reliable but are one-way and relatively slow, allow no re-transmissions, and require high up-front costs ($3000–4000) but no recurrent costs. Communications technology is changing constantly and requires vigilant attention by maintenance personnel.

1.4.6. Quality Assurance and Quality Control

Quality control and quality assurance are issues at every step through the entire sequence of sensing, communication, storage, retrieval, and display of environmental data. Quality assurance is an umbrella concept that covers all data collection and processing (start-to-finish) and ensures that credible information is available to the end user. Quality control has a more limited scope and is defined by the International Standards Organization as "the operational techniques and activities that are used to satisfy quality requirements." The central problem can be better appreciated if we approach quality control in the following way.

- Quality control is the evaluation, assessment, and rehabilitation of imperfect data by utilizing other imperfect data.

The quality of the data only decreases with time once the observation is made. The best and most effective quality control, therefore, consists in making high-quality measurements from the start and then successfully transmitting the measurements to an ingest process and storage site. Once the data are received from a monitoring station, a series of checks with increasing complexity can be applied, ranging from single-element checks (self-consistency) to multiple-element checks (inter-sensor consistency) to multiple-station/single-element checks (inter-station consistency). Suitable ancillary data (battery voltages, data ranges for all measurements, etc.) can prove extremely useful in diagnosing problems.

There is rarely a single technique in quality control procedures that will work satisfactorily for all situations. Quality-control procedures must be tailored to individual station circumstances, data access and storage methods, and climate regimes.

The fundamental issue in quality control centers on the tradeoff between falsely rejecting good data (Type I error) and falsely accepting bad data (Type II error). We cannot reduce the incidence of one type of error without increasing the incidence of the other type. In weather and climate data assessments, since good data are absolutely crucial for interpreting climate records properly, Type I errors are deemed far less desirable than Type II errors.

Not all observations are equal in importance. Quality-control procedures are likely to have the greatest difficulty evaluating the most extreme observations, where independent information usually must be sought and incorporated. Quality-control procedures involving more than one station usually involve a great deal of infrastructure with its own (imperfect) error-detection methods, which must be in place before a single value can be evaluated.

1.4.7. Standards

Although there is near-universal recognition of the value in systematic weather and climate measurements, these measurements will have little value unless they conform to accepted standards. There is not a single source for standards for collecting weather and climate data nor a single standard that meets all needs. Measurement standards have been developed by the American Association of State Climatologists (AASC 1985), U.S. Environmental Protection Agency (EPA 1987), World Meteorological Organization (WMO 1983; 2005), Finklin and Fischer (1990), National Wildfire Coordinating Group (2004), and the RAWS program (Bureau of Land Management [BLM] 1997). Variations to these measurement standards also have been offered by instrument makers (e.g., Tanner 1990).

1.4.8. Who Makes the Measurements?

The lands under NPS stewardship provide many excellent locations to host the monitoring of climate by the NPS or other collaborators. These lands are largely protected from human development and other land changes that can impact observed climate records. Most park units historically have observed weather/climate elements as part of their overall mission. Many of these measurements come from station networks managed by other agencies, with observations taken or overseen by NPS personnel, in some cases, or by collaborators from the other agencies. National Park Service units that are small, lack sufficient resources, or lack sites presenting adequate exposure may benefit by utilizing weather/climate measurements collected from nearly stations.

2.0. Climate Background

Ecosystem processes in the UCBN are strongly governed by climate characteristics (Garrett et al. 2005). It is essential that the UCBN park units have an effective climate monitoring system to track climate changes and to aid in management decisions relating to these changes. These efforts are needed in order to support current vital sign monitoring activities within the park units of the UCBN. In order to do this, however, it is essential to understand the climate characteristics of the UCBN. These characteristics are discussed in this chapter.

2.1. Climate and the UCBN Environment

The UCBN is in a transitional climate zone and climate patterns are dominated by topographic features (Quigley and Arbelbide 1997; Ferguson 1999). Vegetation type and distribution varies depending on the soils, long-term precipitation patterns, and climate. Climate at park sites is influenced by three distinct air masses: 1) moist, marine air from the west that moderates seasonal temperatures; 2) continental air from the east and south, which is dry and cold in winter and hot with convective storms in summer; and 3) dry, arctic air from the north that brings cold air to the basin in winter and helps to cool the basin in summer (Ferguson 1999).

Climate in the UCBN displays variability at a wide range of spatiotemporal scales and, in concert with geology and landforms, exerts the most fundamental driving forces on the distribution, form, and function of UCBN ecosystems. The interaction of latitude, prevailing westerly winds, and topographic variations has created a cool, semi-arid climate that displays significant spatial variability and is characterized by seasonal temperature extremes and highly variable seasonal precipitation patterns (Garrett et al. 2005). Interannual variability in weather and climatic patterns in the UCBN is driven strongly by variations in regional- and global-scale climate indices such as the Pacific Decadal Oscillation (PDO; Mantua et al. 1997; Mantua 2000) and the El Niño Southern Oscillation (ENSO; Redmond and Koch 1991; Mock 1996; Cayan et al. 1998.

Most precipitation accumulates during winter in the UCBN. Mountain snowpack acts as a natural reservoir and supplies the basin with most of its useable water. However, some studies indicate that future climate changes may lead to a general decrease in winter precipitation (Mote et al. 2005) and increase in summer precipitation (Ferguson 1999) in the UCBN.

Temperatures are generally mild in the UCBN because of the periodic influxes of moderating Pacific moisture. Over the past century, some studies have found that winter temperatures have increased slightly while summer temperatures have decreased slightly (Ferguson 1999). In addition to this, climate change scenarios identified by the U.S. Global Change Research Program (USGCRP) for the Rocky Mountain/Great Basin region, including the UCBN, are complex but include a reduction in snowpack and an overall aridification of the region, with increased evapotranspiration negating the effects of potential increased summer precipitation (Wagner et al. 2003).

Historically, the UCBN has been influenced extensively by glaciation events. Repeat events of glaciation during the Pleistocene Epoch reshaped much of the Columbia Plateau. Continental ice sheets reached as far south as the Spokane area in eastern Washington, and montane glaciers reached farther south down the Rocky Mountain and Cascade chains. Massive pluvial lakes and ice dams drove repeated flood events that continue to have a tremendous effect on modern day geomorphology as well as land use practices (Garrett et al. 2005).

Climate models suggest that the Great Basin and Columbia Basin may get warmer and wetter over the next 100 years (Wagner et al. 2003). Predicting effects of global warming for the UCBN are complicated by interactions with global precipitation patterns (most notably, patterns associated with ENSO). Altered precipitation patterns may lead to reduced snowpack and increased summer rain, although a net drying effect, rather than a more mesic summer climate, seems more likely (Melack et al 1997; Wagner et al. 2003). Increases in mean annual temperature and increased temperature extremes may occur, as well as elevated levels of carbon dioxide. Possible ecosystem effects include increased fire frequency and intensity (Heyerdahl et al. 2002; Hessl et al. 2004), increased rates of plant invasions, and increased rates and extents of plant pest outbreaks (D'Antonio 2000; Smith et al. 2000; Logan and Powell 2001; Whitlock et al. 2003; McKenzie et al. 2004).

2.2. Spatial Variability

The overall semi-arid climate characteristics of the UCBN are defined by the region's location between the Cascade Mountains and the northern Rocky Mountains (Garrett et al. 2005). The topographical characteristics of the UCBN introduce significant spatial variability in the region's climate. Mean annual precipitation in the UCBN ranges from just under 250 mm near HAFO up to 750 mm near BIHO and some of the NEPE units.

The timing of the wet season varies dramatically around the UCBN, as the region includes the Columbia Basin and the Snake River Plain, both west of the Continental Divide, as well as some park units in Montana that are either near or east of the Rockies (Figure 1.1). For regions such as the Columbia Basin and the Snake River Plain, the seasonal maximum in precipitation tends to occur in the winter months. This occurs, for example, at CRMO, WHMI, and LARO (Figure 2.1). Winter precipitation in UCBN park units generally amounts to 200-400 mm (Garrett et al. 2005). While slopes on the west sides of the Cascade Mountains receive the heaviest precipitation, the UCBN is positioned largely in the rainshadow of these mountains and receives considerably less precipitation (Figure 2.2). Wintertime precipitation in the UCBN is dominated by non-convective precipitation from winter storms associated with the semi-permanent Aleutian Low, generally positioned in the Gulf of Alaska. Some places within the Columbia Basin and Snake River Plain do, however, have an increase in precipitation during the spring months as well (Figure 2.3). These locations are generally closer to mountains and other higher-elevation zones in the UCBN. In some cases, this springtime maximum dominates the annual precipitation cycle.

Along and east of the Rockies or in the southernmost portions of the UCBN, much of their annual precipitation can occur during the summer months, due to convective thunderstorms (Garrett et al. 2005). In many of these cases, the wettest months are in late spring and summer (Figure 2.4). Little precipitation occurs in these areas during the winter months due to the rainshadowing effects of upstream mountain ranges. The wet-season precipitation in these areas is much more convective in nature, dominated by spring and summer thunderstorms.

Temperatures in the UCBN are influenced primarily by elevation (Figure 2.5). Mean annual temperatures for park units located at the lowest elevations in the UCBN can reach above 10°C. In upper portions of the Columbia Basin and Snake River Plain, however, mean annual temperatures drop to 4-6°C. Temperatures in the eastern portions of the UCBN are also influenced by cold continental and polar air masses moving southward from Canada during the winter months. These air masses primarily influence areas that are at and east of the Rocky Mountains, introducing an east-west temperature gradient with cooler mean annual temperatures occurring in the eastern portion of the UCBN. The coolest park unit is BIHO, which is located in a high valley in the Rocky Mountains of western Montana. The mean annual temperature at BIHO is between 1-2°C.

This east-west gradient in temperature is shown clearly in the January minimum temperatures for the UCBN (Figure 2.6). Winter mean monthly temperatures range from -10°C to -3°C in the UCBN (Garrett et al. 2005) and the coldest mountain valleys in the UCBN, such as at BIHO, can see winter temperatures that regularly drop below -15°C. The most extreme cold-air outbreaks in western Montana have seen temperatures dip much lower, however. For example, Wisdom, Montana, about 20 km east of BIHO, has seen winter temperatures as low as -48°C. Further to the west, where Arctic cold-air outbreaks are relatively less common, mean January minimum temperatures are moderated greatly compared to locations to the east and can be as mild as -4°C in places such as WHMI.

Summer temperatures in the UCBN are largely a function of elevation. The warmest locations in the UCBN are located in the lower portions of the Snake River Plain in southwestern Idaho (Figure 2.7). July maximum temperatures in the lower Snake River Plain commonly exceed 30°C and can get as high as 45°C. However, July maximum temperatures at higher-elevation park units in the UCBN, such as BIHO, do not get much higher than 20°C and freezing temperatures at night are still common.

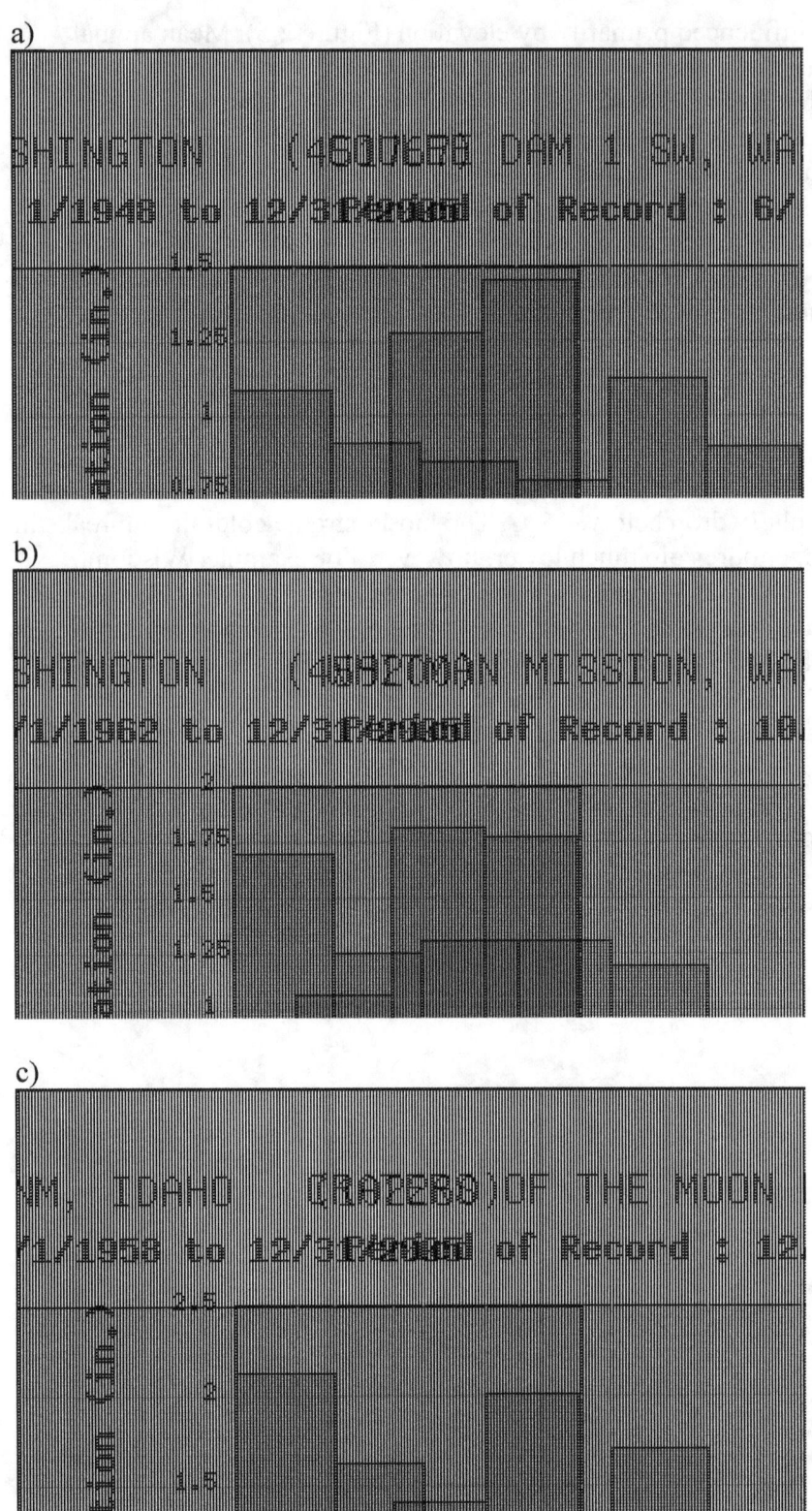

Figure 2.1. Locations in the UCBN with winter precipitation maxima. Locations include Coulee Dam 1 SW, near the south end of LARO (a); WHMI (b); and CRMO (c).

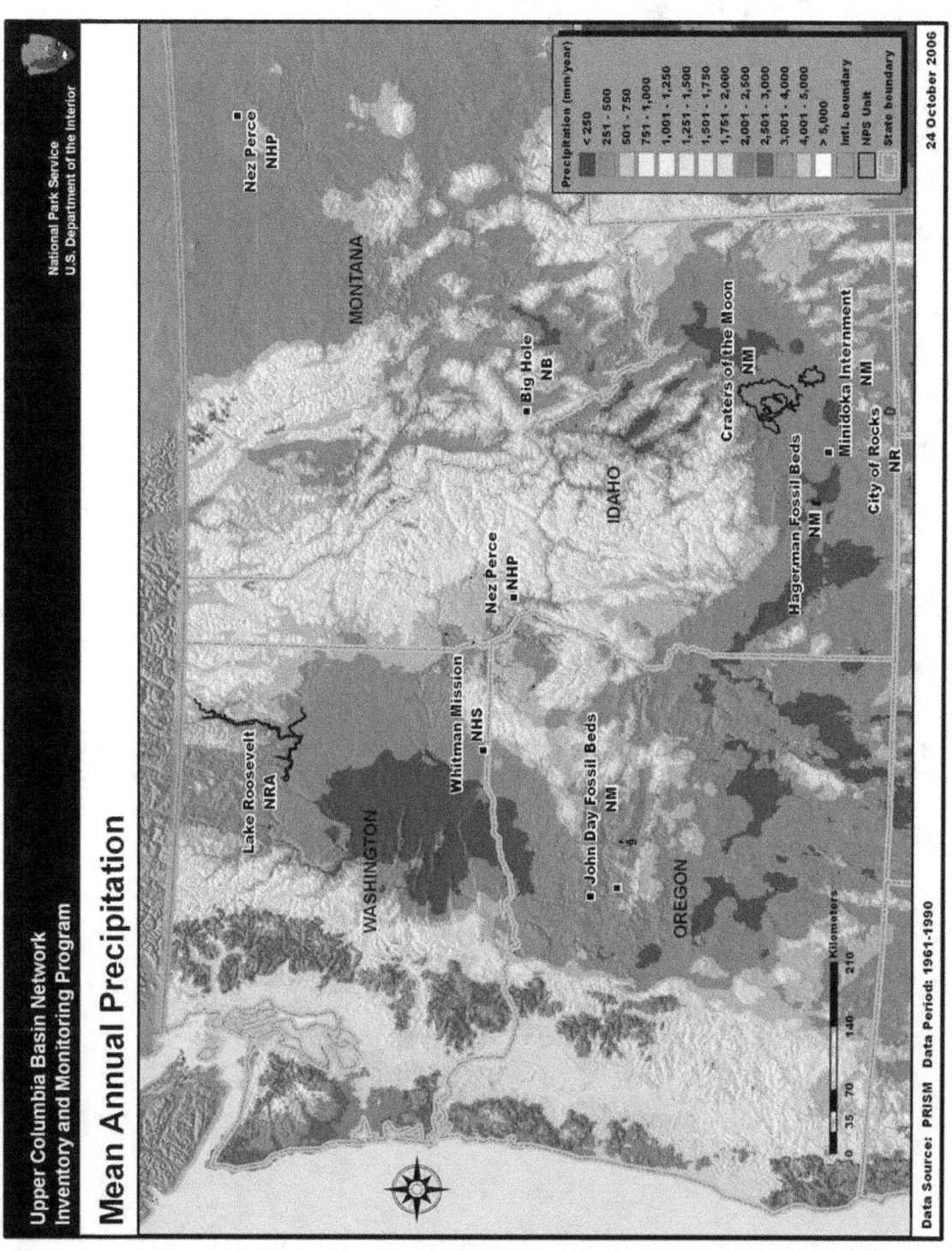

Figure 2.2. Mean annual precipitation, 1961-1990, for the UCBN.

13

a)

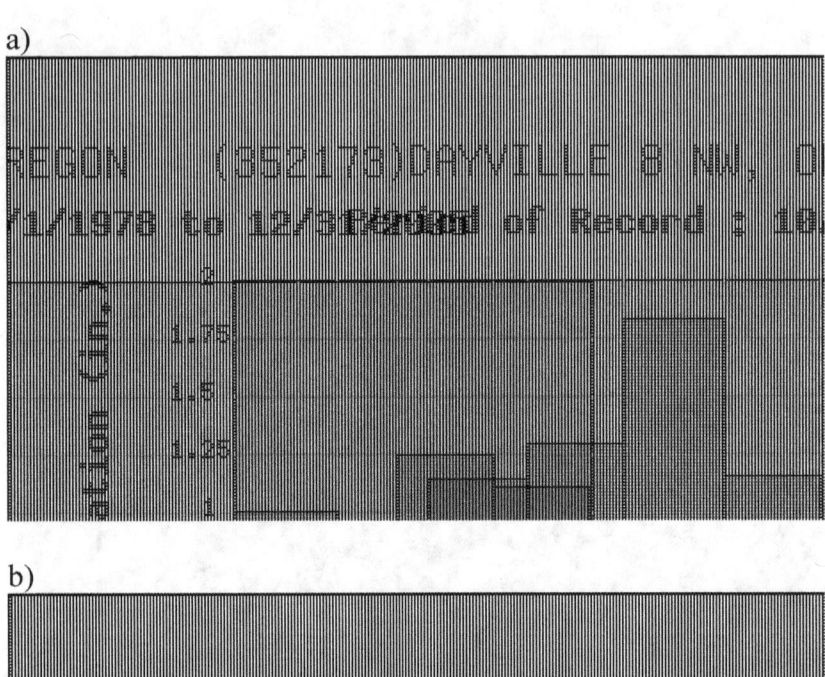

b)

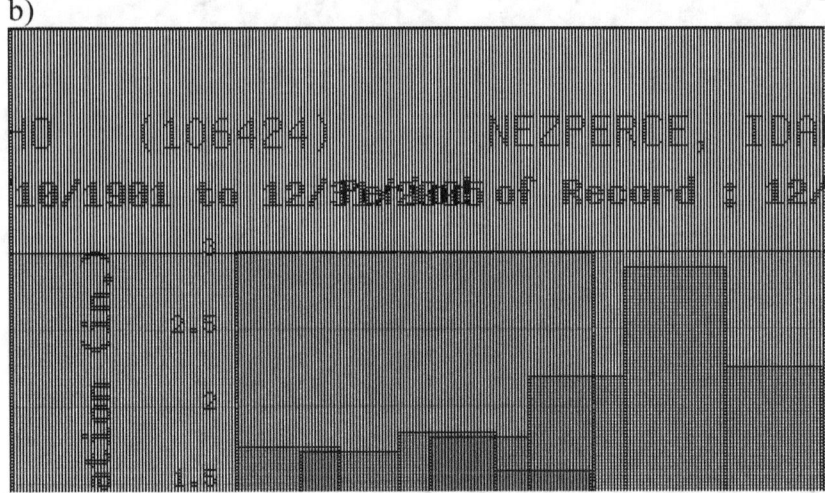

Figure 2.3. Locations in the UCBN with spring precipitation maxima. Sites include Dayville 8 NW (a) and Nezperce (b). Dayville 8 NW is located at the Sheep Rock Unit of JODA, while Nezperce is located just west of the East Kamiah (Heart of the Monster) Unit of NEPE.

a)

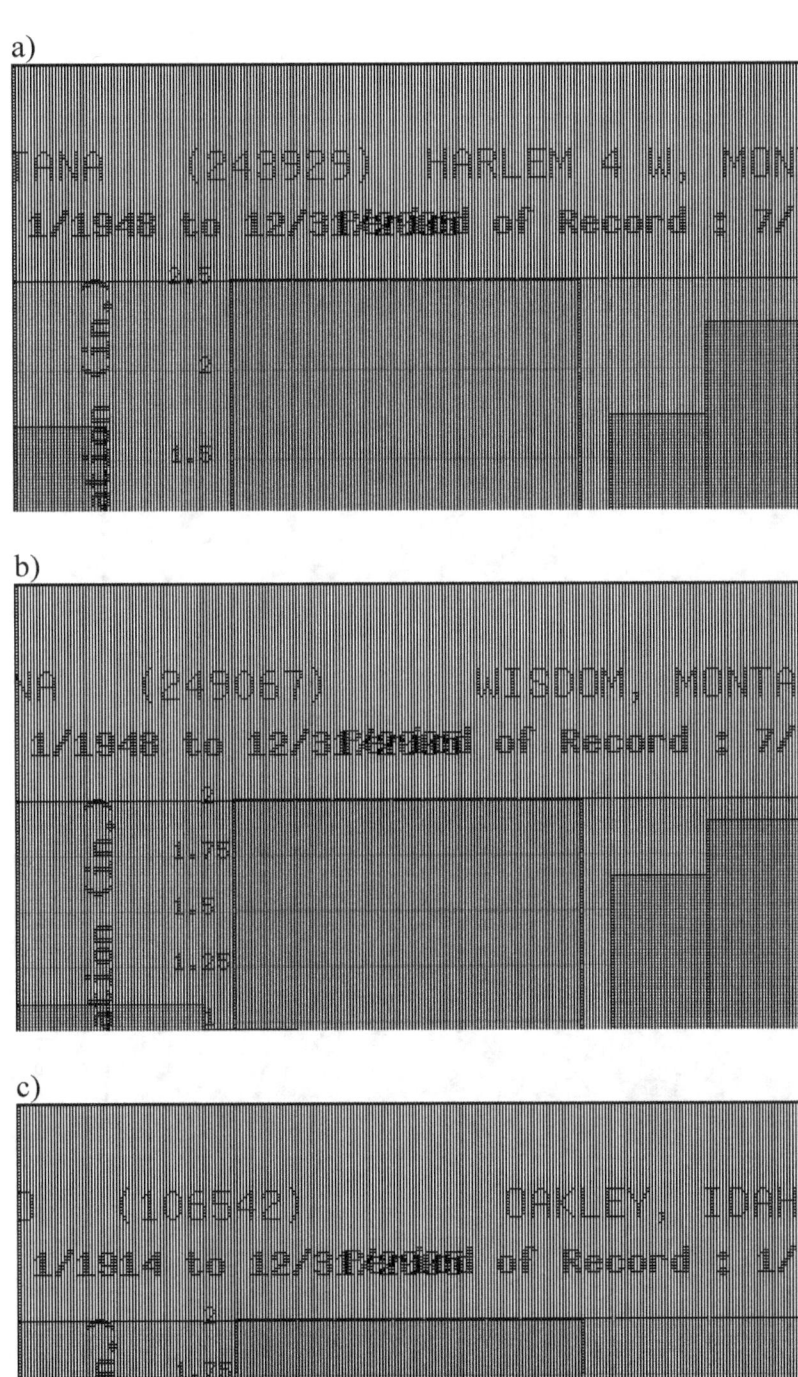

b)

c)

Figure 2.4. Locations in the UCBN with late-spring or summer precipitation maxima. Stations include Harlem 4 W (a), Wisdom (b), and Oakley (c). Harlem 4 W is located northeast of the Bear Paw Battlefield unit of NEPE; Wisdom is located east of BIHO; and Oakley is located northwest of CIRO.

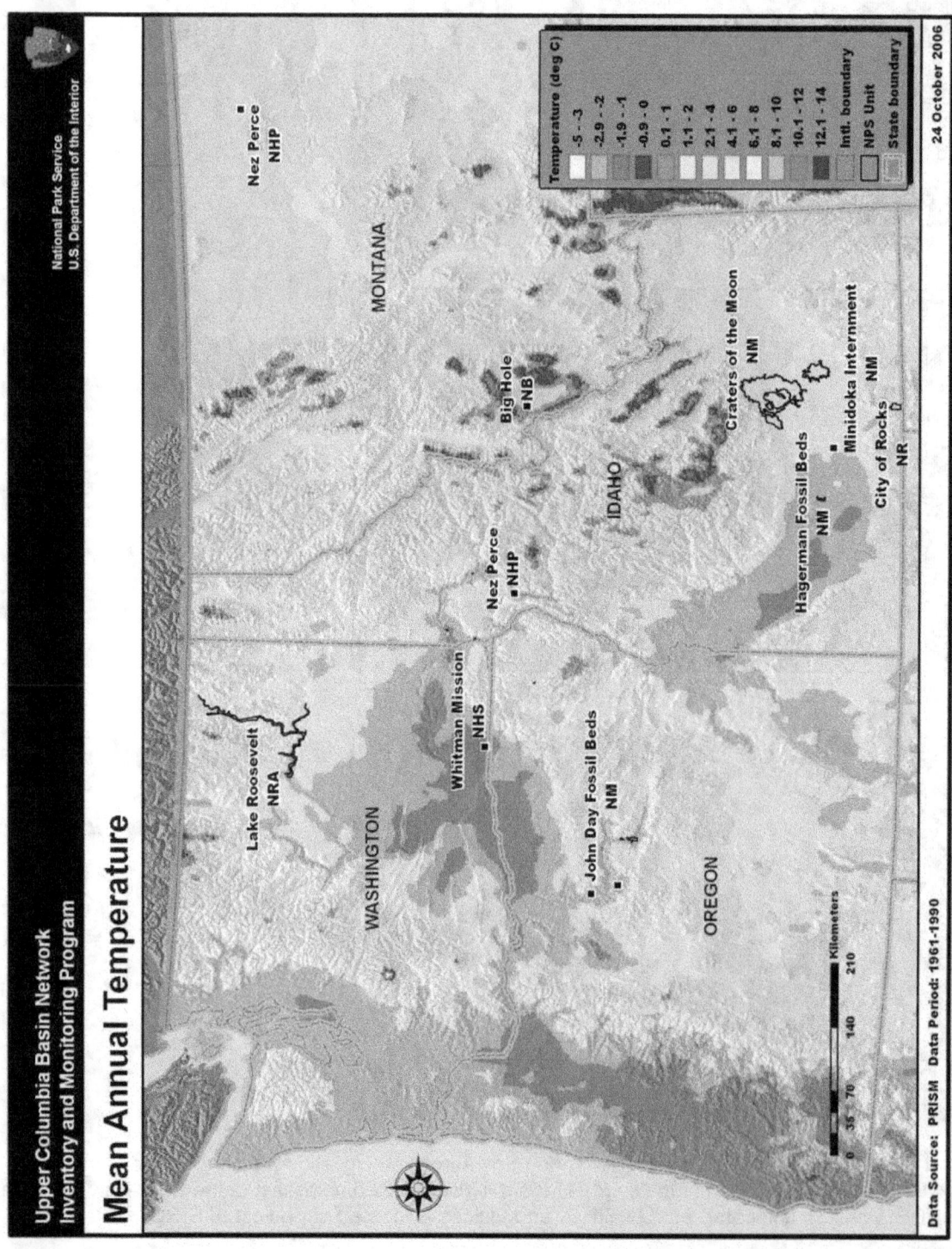

Figure 2.5. Mean annual temperature, 1961-1990, for the UCBN.

16

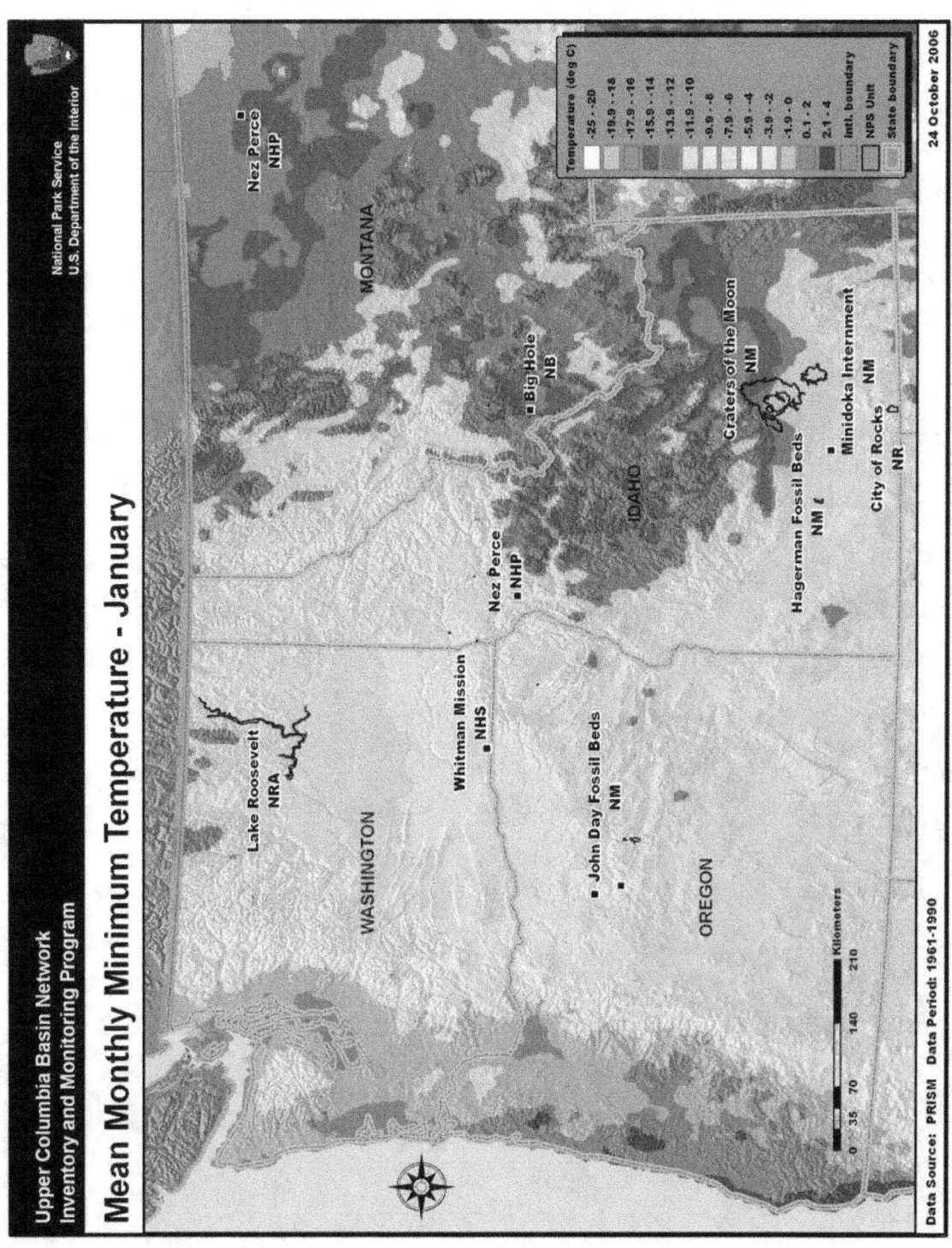

Figure 2.6. Mean January minimum temperature, 1961-1990, for the UCBN.

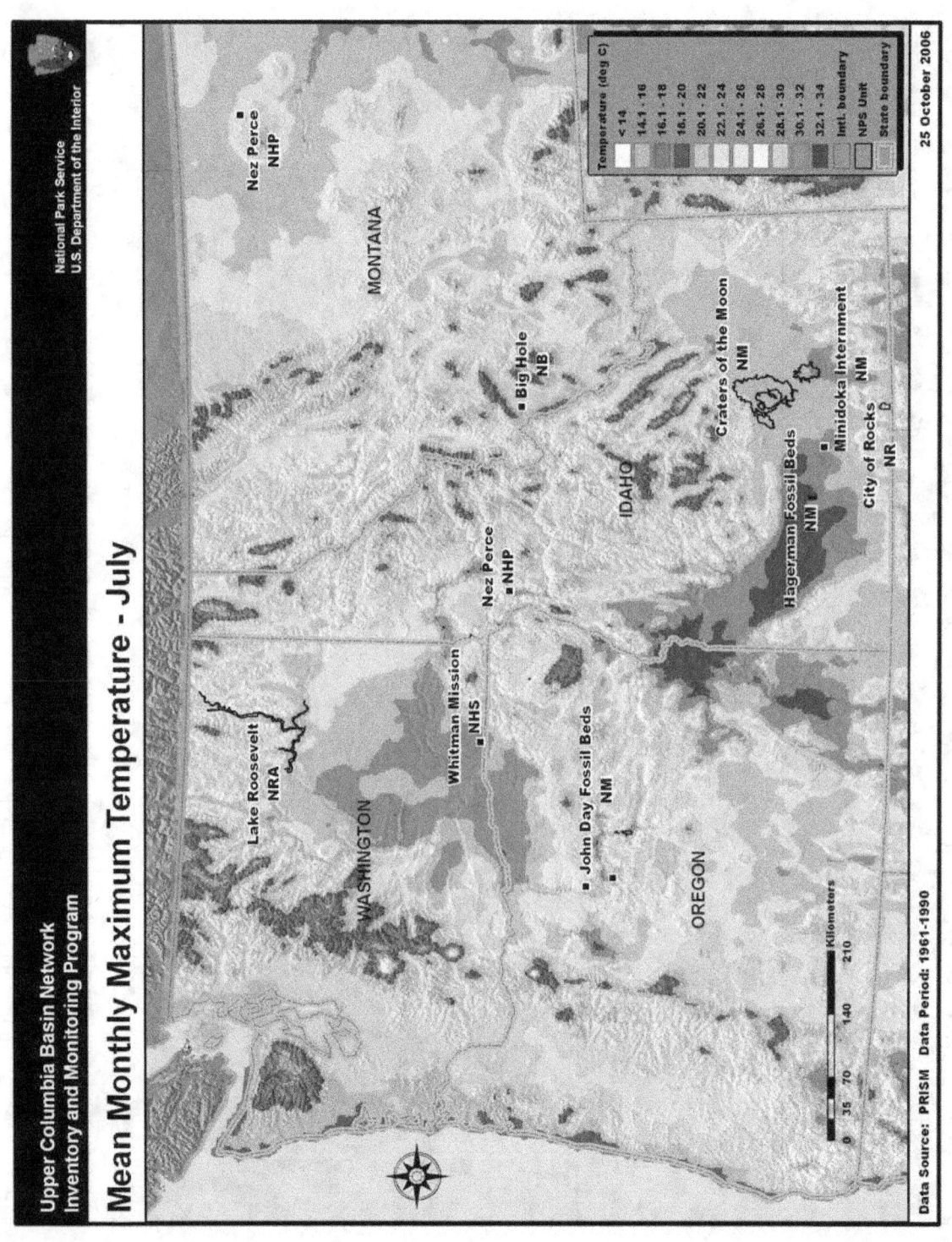

Figure 2.7. Mean July maximum temperature, 1961-1990, for the UCBN.

18

2.3. Temporal Variability

The Pacific-North America Oscillation (PNA; Wallace and Gutzler 1981) is an important contributor to variability of storm frequencies and tracks during a given year, with variations that occur on the order of weeks. Negative phases of the PNA are generally associated with cooler temperatures and increased storminess over the UCBN, particularly in those areas west of the Rockies.

Both the El Niño Southern Oscillation (ENSO) and the Pacific Decadal Oscillation (PDO) cause interannual climate variations in the UCBN (Redmond and Koch 1991; Mock 1996; Mantua et al. 1997; Cayan et al. 1998; Mantua et al. 2000; NAST 2001) with corresponding impacts on the natural systems of the UCBN (Heyerdahl et al. 2002; Hessl et al. 2004; Mote et al. 2005). El Niño conditions and/or positive phases of the PDO are associated with warmer and drier than normal conditions in the UCBN, while La Niña conditions and/or negative phases of the PDO are associated with cooler and wetter than normal conditions.

Precipitation time series in the region do not appear to show any significant trend (Figure 2.8). However, some studies do indicate seasonal trends in precipitation in the last 50 to 100 years, including a general decrease in winter precipitation and increase in summer precipitation (Ferguson 1999).

Long-term temperature time series, however, do show some warming, particularly in the last 2-3 decades (Figure 2.9). It is estimated that surface temperatures in the northwestern U.S. have warmed by 1-3°C over the last century (NAST 2001). Seasonally, some studies have found that temperature trends in the last 50 to 100 years show a slight increase in winter temperatures and a slight decrease in summer temperatures (Ferguson 1999).

2.4. Parameter Regression on Independent Slopes Model

The climate maps presented here were generated using the Parameter Regression on Independent Slopes Model (PRISM). This model is maintained by PRISM Group at Oregon State University (http://www.ocs.orst.edu/prism) and was developed to address the extreme spatial and elevation gradients exhibited by the climate of the western U.S. (Daly et al. 1994; 2002; Gibson et al. 2002; Doggett et al. 2004). Originally, this model was developed to describe spatial climate variability at scales that match available land-cover maps, to assist in ecologic modeling. Spatial climate data sets generated from PRISM are now widely used for Geographic Information Systems applications. The PRISM technique accounts for the scale-dependent effects of topography on mean values of climate elements. Elevation provides the first-order constraint for the mapped climate fields, with slope and orientation (aspect) providing second-order constraints. The model has been enhanced gradually to address inversions, coast/land gradients, and climate patterns in small-scale trapping basins. Monthly climate fields are generated by PRISM to account for seasonal variations in elevation gradients in climate elements. These monthly climate fields then can be combined into seasonal and annual climate fields. Since PRISM maps are grid maps, they do not replicate point values but rather, for a given grid cell, represent the grid-cell average of the climate variable in question at the average elevation for that cell. The model relies on observed surface and upper-air measurements to estimate spatial climate fields.

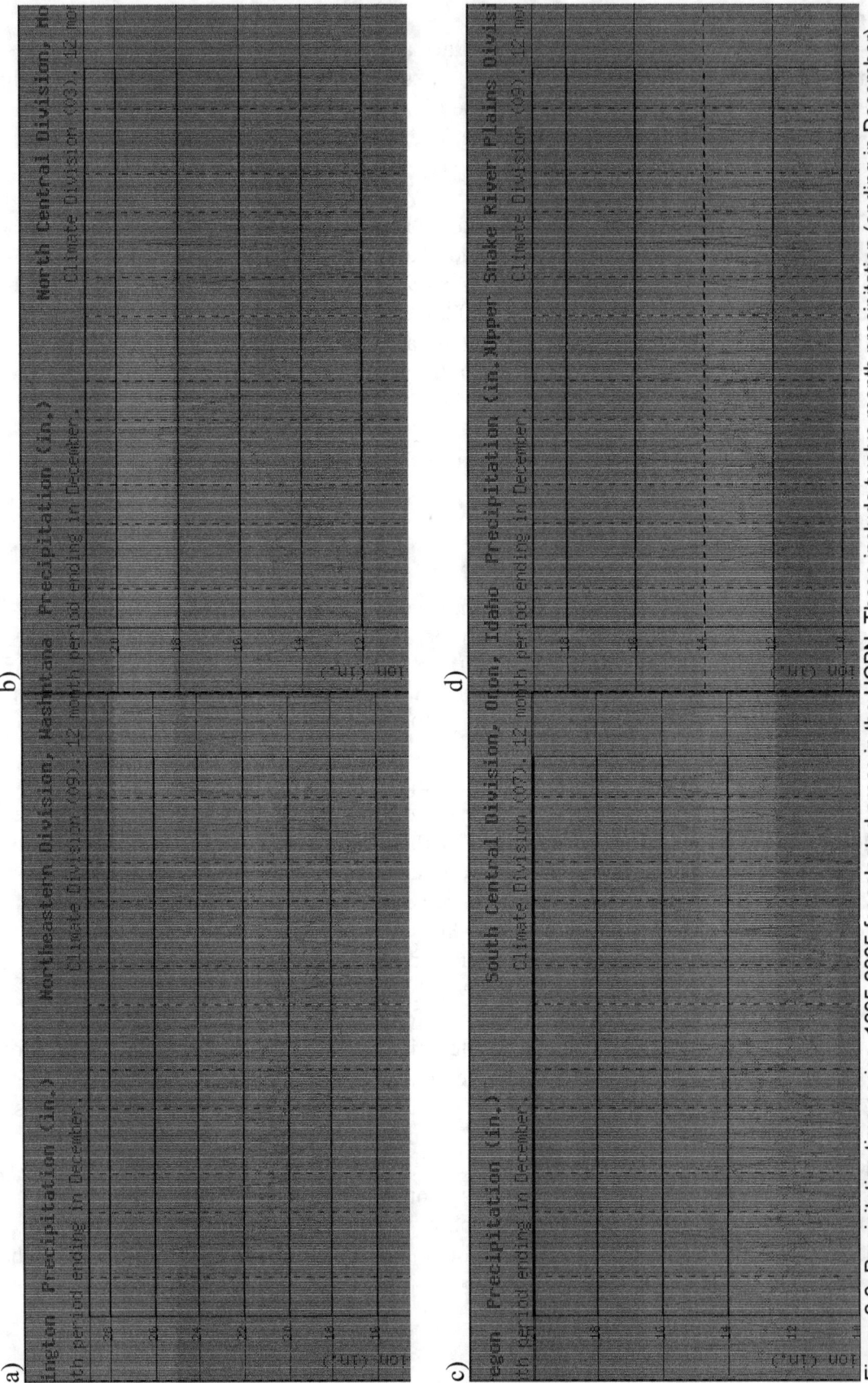

Figure 2.8. Precipitation time series, 1895-2005 for selected areas in the UCBN. These include twelve-month precipitation (ending in December) (red), 10-year running mean (blue), mean (green), and plus/minus one standard deviation (green dotted). Areas include northeastern Washington (a), north-central Montana (b), south-central Oregon (c), and the upper Snake River Plain in Idaho (d).

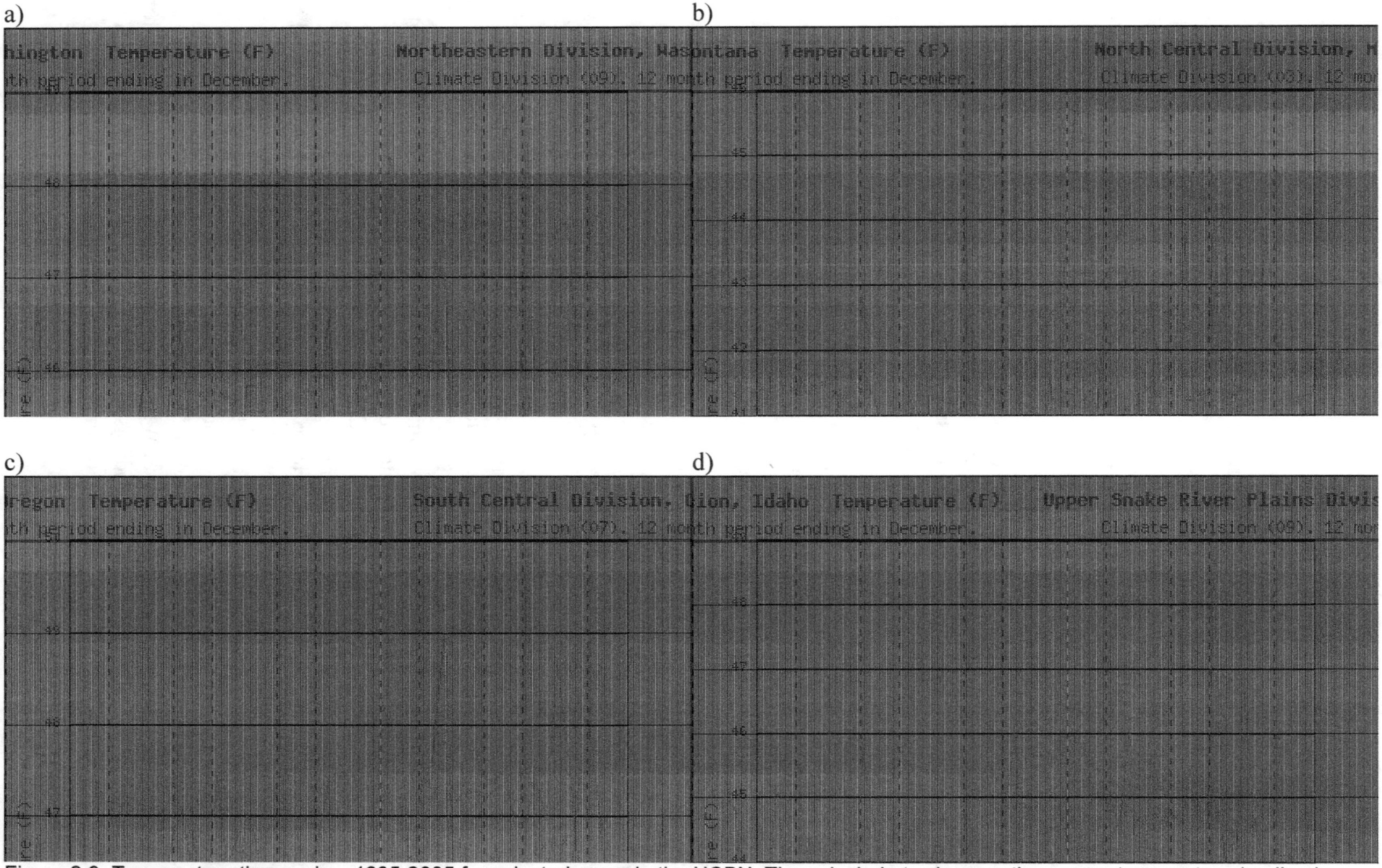

Figure 2.9. Temperature time series, 1895-2005 for selected areas in the UCBN. These include twelve-month average temperature (ending in December) (red), 10-year running mean (blue), mean (green), and plus/minus one standard deviation (green dotted). Areas include northeastern Washington (a), north-central Montana (b), south-central Oregon (c), and the upper Snake River Plain in Idaho (d).

3.0. Methods

Having discussed the climatic characteristics of the UCBN, we now present the procedures that were used to obtain information for weather/climate stations within the UCBN. This information was obtained from various sources, as mentioned in the following paragraphs. Retrieval of station metadata constituted a major component of this work.

3.1. Metadata Retrieval

A key component of station inventories is determining the kinds of observations that have been conducted over time, by whom, and in what manner; when each type of observation began and ended; and whether these observations are still being conducted. Metadata about the observational process (Table 3.1) generally consist of a series of vignettes that apply to time intervals and, therefore, constitute a *history* rather than a single snapshot. An expanded list of relevant metadata fields for this inventory is provided in Appendix D. This report has relied on metadata records from three sources: (a) Western Regional Climate Center (WRCC), (b) NPS personnel, and (c) other knowledgeable personnel, such as state climate office staff.

The metadata sources for this report were stored at WRCC. This regional climate center (RCC) acts as a working repository of many western climate records, including the main networks outlined in this section. Live and periodic ingests from all major national and western weather/climate networks are maintained at WRCC. These networks include the COOP network, the Surface Airways Observation Network (SAO) jointly operated by NOAA and the Federal Aviation Administration (FAA), the NOAA upper-air observation network, NOAA data buoys, the RAWS network, the SNOTEL network, and various smaller networks. The WRCC is expanding its capability to ingest information from other networks as resources permit and usefulness dictates. This center has relied heavily on historic archives (in many cases supplemented with live ingests) to assess the quantity (not necessarily quality) of data available for NPS I&M network applications.

The primary source of metadata at WRCC is the Applied Climate Information System (ACIS), a joint effort among RCCs and other NOAA entities. Metadata for UCBN weather/climate stations identified from the ACIS database are available in file "UCBN_from_ACIS.tar.gz" (see Appendix G). Historic metadata pertaining to major climate- and weather-observing systems in the United States are stored in ACIS where metadata are linked to the observed data. A distributed system, ACIS is synchronized among the RCCs. Mainstream software is utilized, including Postgress, Python™, and Java™ programming languages; CORBA®-compliant network software; and industry-standard, nonproprietary hardware and software. Metadata and data for all major national climate and weather networks have been entered into the ACIS database. The available metadata from many smaller networks also have been entered but in most cases the data from these smaller networks have not yet been entered. Data sets are in the NetCDF (Network Common Data Form) format, but the design allows for integration with legacy systems, including non-NetCDF files (used at WRCC) and additional metadata (added for this project). The ACIS also supports a suite of products to visualize or summarize data from these data sets. National climate-monitoring maps are updated daily using the ACIS data feed.

Table 3.1. Primary metadata fields for weather/climate stations within the UCBN. Explanations are provided as appropriate.

Metadata Field	Notes
Station name	Station name associated with network listed in "Climate Network."
Latitude	Numerical value (units: see coordinate units).
Longitude	Numerical value (units: see coordinate units).
Coordinate units	Latitude/longitude (units: decimal degrees, degree-minute-second, etc.).
Datum	Datum used as basis for coordinates: WGS 84, NAD 83, etc.
Elevation	Elevation of station above mean sea level (m).
Slope	Slope of ground surface below station (degrees).
Aspect	Azimuth that ground surface below station faces.
Climate division	NOAA climate division where station is located. Climate divisions are NOAA-specified zones sharing similar climate and hydrology characteristics.
Country	Country where station is located.
State	State where station is located.
County	County where station is located.
Weather/climate network	Primary weather/climate network the station belongs to (COOP, RAWS, etc.).
NPS unit code	Four-letter code identifying park unit where station resides.
NPS unit name	Full name of park unit.
NPS unit type	National park, national monument, etc.
UTM zone	If UTM is the only coordinate system available.
Location notes	Useful information not already included in "station narrative."
Climate variables	Temperature, precipitation, etc.
Installation date	Date of station installation.
Removal date	Date of station removal.
Station photograph	Digital image of station.
Photograph date	Date photograph was taken.
Photographer	Name of person who took the photograph.
Station narrative	Anything related to general site description; may include site exposure, characteristics of surrounding vegetation, driving directions, etc.
Contact name	Name of the person involved with station operation.
Organization	Group or agency affiliation of contact person.
Contact type	Designation that identifies contact person as the station owner, observer, maintenance person, data manager, etc.
Position/job title	Official position/job title of contact person.
Address	Address of contact person.
E-mail address	E-mail address of contact person.
Phone	Phone number of contact person (and extension if available).
Contact notes	Other information needed to reach contact person.

The developmental phases of ACIS have utilized metadata supplied by the NCDC and NWS. These metadata include many tens of thousands of entries, screened as well as possible for duplications, mistakes, and omissions.

Two types of information have been used to complete the climate station inventory for UCBN.

- <u>Station inventories</u>: Information about observational procedures, latitude/longitude, elevation, measured elements, measurement frequency, sensor types, exposures, ground cover and vegetation, data-processing details, network, purpose, and managing individual or agency, etc.

- <u>Data inventories</u>: Information about measured data values including completeness, seasonality, data gaps, representation of missing data, flagging systems, how special circumstances in the data record are denoted, etc.

This is not a straightforward process. Extensive searches are typically required to develop historic station and data inventories. Both types of inventories frequently contain information gaps and often rely on tacit and unrealistic assumptions. Sources of information for these inventories frequently are difficult to recover or are undocumented and unreliable. In many cases, the actual weather/climate data available from different sources are not linked directly to metadata records. To the extent that actual data can be acquired (rather than just metadata), it is possible to cross-check these records and perform additional assessments based on the amount and completeness of the data.

Certain types of weather/climate networks that possess any of the following attributes have not been considered for inclusion in the inventory:

- Private networks with proprietary access and/or inability to obtain or provide sufficient metadata.
- Private weather enthusiasts (often with high-quality data) whose metadata are not available and whose data are not readily accessible.
- Unofficial observers supplying data to the NWS (lack of access to current data and historic archives; lack of metadata).
- Networks having no available historic data.
- Networks having poor-quality metadata.
- Networks having poor access to metadata.
- Real-time networks having poor access to real-time data.

Previous inventory efforts at WRCC have shown that for the weather networks identified in the preceding list, in light of the need for quality data to track weather and climate, the resources required and difficulty encountered in obtaining metadata or data are prohibitively large.

3.2. Criteria for Locating Stations

To identify stations for each park unit in UCBN, we selected all weather and climate stations, past and present, which were located inside UCBN park units or within 40 km of a UCBN park-unit boundary. We selected a 40-km buffer in order to ensure the inclusion of a sufficient number of both manual and automated stations in and near the park units in the UCBN.

The station locator maps presented in Chapter 4 were designed to show clearly the spatial distributions of all major weather/climate station networks in UCBN. We recognize that other mapping formats may be more suitable for other specific needs.

24

4.0. Station Inventory

An objective of this report is to show the locations of weather/climate stations for the UCBN region in relation to the boundaries of the NPS park units within UCBN. A station does not have to be within park boundaries to provide useful data and information for a park unit.

4.1. Climate and Weather Networks

Most stations in the UCBN are associated with one of at least 18 weather/climate networks (Table 4.1). Brief descriptions of each weather/climate network are provided below (see Appendix F for greater detail).

Table 4.1. Weather/climate networks represented within the UCBN.

Acronym	Name
AgriMet	Pacific Northwest Cooperative Agricultural Network
ARL FRD	NOAA Air Resources Laboratory Field Research Division
CANADA	Canadian weather/climate stations
COOP	NWS Cooperative Observer Program
CWOP	Citizen Weather Observer Program
GPMP	NPS Gaseous Pollutant Monitoring Program
ITD	Idaho Transportation Department network
KBCI	KBCI TV, Boise, Idaho
MCSCN	Montana Counties Soil Climate Network
MSOWFO	NWS Forecast Office, Missoula, Montana
NRCS-SC	USDA/NRCS Snowcourse network
ODOT	Oregon Department of Transportation network
PDTWFO	NWS Forecast Office, Pendleton, Oregon
RAWS	Remote Automated Weather Station network
SAO	NWS/FAA Surface Airways Observation network
SNOTEL	USDA/NRCS Snowfall Telemetry network
UPR	Union Pacific Railroad network
WA DOT	Washington State Department of Transportation network

4.1.1. Pacific Northwest Cooperative Agricultural Network (AgriMet)

AgriMet is a network of automated weather stations operated by the U.S. Bureau of Reclamation. The stations in AgriMet are located primarily in irrigated agricultural areas throughout the Pacific Northwest.

4.1.2. NOAA Air Resources Laboratory Field Research Division (ARL FRD)

The mission of the ARL FRD is to improve understanding of atmospheric transport, atmospheric dispersion, and air-surface exchange processes. One responsibility of the ARL FRD, particular to the UCBN, is to support the Department of Energy's Idaho National Laboratory by providing meteorological forecasts and emergency response capabilities. Meteorological observations at these sites generally include temperature, precipitation, humidity, wind, and solar radiation.

4.1.3. Canadian Weather/Climate Stations (CANADA)

These include various automated weather/climate station networks from Canada. The Meteorological Service of Canada operates many of these stations, including airport sites. The data measured at these sites generally include temperature, precipitation, humidity, wind, pressure, sky cover, ceiling, visibility, and current weather. Most of the data records are of high quality.

4.1.4. NWS Cooperative Observer Program (COOP)

The COOP network has been a foundation of the U.S. climate program for decades and continues to play an important role. Manual measurements are made by volunteers and consist of daily maximum and minimum temperatures, observation-time temperature, daily precipitation, daily snowfall, and snow depth. When blended with NWS measurements, the data set is known as SOD, or "Summary of the Day." The quality of data from COOP sites ranges from excellent to modest.

4.1.5. Citizen Weather Observer Program (CWOP)

The CWOP network consists primarily of automated weather stations operated by private citizens who have either an Internet connection and/or a wireless Ham radio setup. Data from CWOP stations are specifically intended for use in research, education, and homeland security activities. Although meteorological elements such as temperature, precipitation, and wind are measured at all CWOP stations, station characteristics do vary, including sensor types and site exposure.

4.1.6. NPS Gaseous Pollutant Monitoring Program (GPMP)

The GPMP network measures hourly meteorological data in support of pollutant monitoring activities. Measured elements include temperature, precipitation, humidity, wind, solar radiation, and surface wetness. These data are generally of high quality, with records extending up to 1-2 decades in length.

4.1.7. Idaho Department of Transportation Network (ITD)

These weather stations are operated by ITD in support of management activities for Idaho's transportation network. Measured meteorological elements include temperature, precipitation, wind, and relative humidity.

4.1.8. KBCI TV, Boise, Idaho (KBCI)

Weather stations in this network are operated by volunteers supported by KBCI TV in Boise, Idaho. These stations provide near-real-time data to KBCI in support of KBCI's daily weather segments on their daily news programs. Measured meteorological elements include temperature, precipitation, wind, and relative humidity.

4.1.9. Montana Counties Soil Climate Network (MCSCN)

This network was initiated in response to the need to monitor drought conditions in the state of Montana. This network provides near-real-time information on rainfall and soil moisture, along with any other data that is useful for drought assistance. Soil moisture and temperature measurements are taken at depths of 6, 12, 18, and 30 inches (15, 30, 46, and 76 cm). Measured meteorological elements include temperature, precipitation, wind speed and direction.

4.1.10. NWS Forecast Office, Missoula, Montana (MSOWFO)
These are near-real-time stations managed by the NWS forecast office in Missoula, Montana. Data from these stations are used to provide local weather data to assist in developing routine weather forecasts for western Montana. Measured meteorological elements include temperature, precipitation, wind, and relative humidity.

4.1.11. USDA/NRCS Snowcourse Network (NRCS-SC)
The USDA/NRCS maintains a network of snow-monitoring stations known as snowcourses. These are all manual sites, measuring only snow depth and snow water content one–two times per month during the months of January to June. Data records for these snowcourses often extend back to the 1920s or 1930s, and the data are generally of high quality. Many of these sites have been replaced by SNOTEL sites, but several hundred snowcourses are still in operation.

4.1.12. Oregon Department of Transportation Network (ODOT)
These weather stations are operated by ODOT in support of management activities for Oregon's transportation network. Measured meteorological elements include temperature, precipitation, wind, and relative humidity.

4.1.13. NWS Forecast Office, Pendleton, Oregon (PDTWFO)
These are near-real-time stations managed by the NWS forecast office in Pendleton, Oregon. Data from these stations are used to provide local weather data to assist in developing routine weather forecasts for central and eastern Oregon. Measured meteorological elements include temperature, precipitation, wind, and relative humidity.

4.1.14. Remote Automated Weather Station Network (RAWS)
The RAWS network is administered through many land management agencies, particularly the BLM and the Forest Service. Hourly meteorology elements are measured and include temperature, wind, humidity, solar radiation, barometric pressure, fuel temperature, and precipitation (when temperatures are above freezing). The fire community is the primary client for RAWS data. These sites are remote and data typically are transmitted via GOES (Geostationary Operational Environmental Satellite). Some sites operate all winter. Most data records for RAWS sites began during or after the mid-1980s.

4.1.15. NWS/FAA Surface Airways Observation Network (SAO)
These stations are located usually at major airports and military bases. Almost all SAO sites are automated. The hourly data measured at these sites include temperature, precipitation, humidity, wind, pressure, sky cover, ceiling, visibility, and current weather. Most data records begin during or after the 1940s, and these data are generally of high quality.

4.1.16. USDA/NRCS Snowfall Telemetry (SNOTEL) Network
The USDA/NRCS maintains a network of automated snow-monitoring stations known as SNOTEL. The network was implemented originally to measure daily precipitation and snow

water content. Many modern SNOTEL sites now record hourly data, with some sites now recording temperature and snow depth. Most data records began during or after the mid-1970s.

4.1.17. Union Pacific Railroad Network (UPR)
This is a network of weather stations managed by UPR to support their shipping and transport activities, primarily in the central and western U.S. These stations are generally located along the UPR's main railroad lines. Measured meteorological elements include temperature, precipitation, wind, and relative humidity.

4.1.18. Washington State Department of Transportation Network (WA DOT)
These weather stations are operated by the Washington State Department of Transportation in support of management activities for Washington's transportation network. Measured meteorological elements include temperature, precipitation, wind, and relative humidity.

4.1.19. Weather Bureau Army Navy (WBAN)
This is a station identification system rather than a true weather/climate network and is not discussed in Appendix F. A brief description of WBAN is provided here. Stations identified with WBAN are largely historical stations that reported meteorological observations on the WBAN weather observation forms that were common during the early and middle parts of the 20th Century. The use of WBAN numbers to identify stations was one of the first attempts in the U.S. to use a coordinated station numbering scheme between several weather station networks, such as the SAO and COOP networks.

4.1.20. Other Networks
In addition to the major networks mentioned above, there are various networks that are operated for specific purposes by specific organizations or governmental agencies or scientific research projects. These networks could be present within UCBN but have not been identified in this report. Some of the commonly used networks include the following:

- NOAA upper-air stations
- National Atmospheric Deposition Program (NADP)
- Federal and state departments of transportation
- National Science Foundation Long-Term Ecologic Research Network
- U.S. Department of Energy Surface Radiation Budget Network (Surfrad)
- U.S. Geological Survey (USGS) hydrologic stations
- Park-specific-monitoring networks and stations
- Other research or project networks having many possible owners

4.2. Station Locations
Only a few park units in the UCBN have weather/climate stations within their boundaries from the networks discussed in Section 4.1 (Table 4.2). The park units with the greatest number of stations are CRMO (five) and LARO (five). Most of these are COOP stations.

Table 4.2. Number of stations within and nearby UCBN park units. Numbers are listed by park unit and by weather/climate network. Figures in parentheses indicate number of stations within park boundaries.

Network	BIHO	CIRO	CRMO	HAFO	JODA	LARO	MIIN	NEPE	WHMI
AgriMet	0(0)	0(0)	1(0)	0(0)	0(0)	0(0)	2(0)	1(0)	0(0)
ARL FRD	0(0)	0(0)	20(1)	0(0)	0(0)	0(0)	0(0)	0(0)	0(0)
CANADA	0(0)	0(0)	0(0)	0(0)	0(0)	1(0)	0(0)	0(0)	0(0)
COOP	12(0)	9(0)	57(2)	11(0)	28(2)	35(4)	13(0)	89(1)	24(1)
CWOP	0(0)	0(0)	2(0)	2(0)	4(0)	6(0)	0(0)	10(0)	8(0)
GPMP	0(0)	0(0)	1(1)	0(0)	0(0)	0(0)	0(0)	0(0)	0(0)
ITD	0(0)	0(0)	8(0)	1(0)	0(0)	0(0)	3(0)	4(0)	0(0)
KBCI	0(0)	0(0)	0(0)	0(0)	0(0)	0(0)	0(0)	1(0)	0(0)
MCSCN	0(0)	0(0)	0(0)	0(0)	0(0)	0(0)	0(0)	1(0)	0(0)
MSOWFO	1(0)	0(0)	0(0)	0(0)	0(0)	0(0)	0(0)	2(0)	0(0)
NRCS-SC	8(0)	5(0)	8(0)	0(0)	4(0)	16(0)	0(0)	13(0)	1(0)
ODOT	0(0)	0(0)	0(0)	0(0)	5(0)	0(0)	0(0)	0(0)	0(0)
PDTWFO	0(0)	0(0)	0(0)	0(0)	7(0)	0(0)	0(0)	0(0)	1(0)
RAWS	4(0)	1(0)	9(1)	1(0)	8(0)	17(1)	1(0)	23(0)	0(0)
SAO	0(0)	2(0)	7(0)	3(0)	0(0)	5(0)	2(0)	6(0)	1(0)
SNOTEL	3(0)	2(0)	4(0)	0(0)	2(0)	0(0)	0(0)	5(0)	0(0)
UPR	0(0)	0(0)	7(0)	2(0)	0(0)	0(0)	2(0)	0(0)	0(0)
WA DOT	0(0)	0(0)	0(0)	0(0)	0(0)	11(0)	0(0)	1(0)	0(0)
Other	0(0)	0(0)	1(0)	0(0)	1(0)	2(0)	1(0)	0(0)	1(0)
Total	28(0)	44(0)	125(5)	20(0)	59(2)	93(5)	24(0)	156(1)	36(1)

4.2.1. Big Hole National Battlefield

No weather/climate stations are located within BIHO (Table 4.3). We have identified eight active COOP stations within 40 km of BIHO. The COOP station "Wisdom," which is about 20 km east of BIHO (Figure 4.1), has the longest record of these active COOP stations, going back to 1923. The data record from this station is very complete with the exception of a one-month gap in January, 1981. The COOP station "Gibbons Pass" is located about 20 km northwest of BIHO and has a data record going back to 1948. The COOP station "Jackson" is located about 35 km southeast of BIHO and also has a data record going back to 1948. However, this station has some significant data gaps in its record. A major data gap occurred at "Jackson" from 1971 to 1978 and scattered multi-month gaps occurred at this same station during the 1980s. Besides the COOP station at Wisdom, the station "Sula 3 ENE" also provides a largely complete data record for the BIHO region. This station has been active since 1955 and the only notable data gaps are in January-April, 1967 and June, 1974. However, although "Sula 3 ENE" is located only 30 km northwest of BIHO, its data may not be representative of the Big Hole Valley, as the station is located across the Anaconda Range from BIHO.

We have identified five automated stations providing near-real-time weather data within 40 km of BIHO (Table 4.3; Figure 4.1). Three of these stations are RAWS stations. The longest record among these stations is found at "Kriley Creek" (1990-present). However, this station is located in the Salmon River Valley, 40 km southwest of BIHO, and thus may not be representative of BIHO. The two other active RAWS stations we identified, "Sula" and "Tepee Point," are each across the Anaconda Range from BIHO and thus may also not be representative of the climate in the Big Hole Valley. The most representative near-real-time weather data for BIHO could come from the SNOTEL station "Calvert Creek," which is one of the two SNOTEL stations we identified within 40 km of BIHO. "Calvert Creek" is located in the Big Hole Valley, about 35 km downstream (northeast) of BIHO.

Table 4.3. Weather/climate stations for BIHO. Stations inside BIHO and within 40 km of the BIHO boundary are included. Missing entries are indicated by "M".

Big Hole National Battlefield – BIHO							
Name	Lat.	Lon.	Elev. (m)	Network	Start	End	In Park?
Conner 5 SE	45.867	-114.050	1305	COOP	8/1/1971	1/7/1976	NO
Gibbons Pass	45.693	-113.955	2134	COOP	7/1/1948	Present	NO
Gibbonsville	45.539	-113.928	1366	COOP	1/1/1895	Present	NO
Gibbonsville No 2	45.547	-113.926	1366	COOP	11/15/2004	Present	NO
Jackson	45.368	-113.409	1975	COOP	6/1/1949	Present	NO
Mc Cart Lookout	45.883	-113.717	2166	COOP	7/1/1956	Present	NO
Moose Creek	45.650	-113.833	1891	COOP	10/1/1966	9/30/1976	NO
Sula 14 NE	45.911	-113.738	1573	COOP	8/3/2001	Present	NO
Sula 3 ENE	45.848	-113.927	1364	COOP	11/30/1955	Present	NO
Wisdom	45.618	-113.451	1847	COOP	1/1/1923	Present	NO
Wise River 17 WNW	45.883	-113.267	1830	COOP	4/1/1955	11/30/1959	NO
Wise River 18 WNW	45.883	-113.300	1922	COOP	10/1/1953	4/30/1955	NO
Laird Creek near Sula	45.870	-114.050	1294	MSOWFO	M	Present	NO

Big Hole National Battlefield – BIHO

Name	Lat.	Lon.	Elev. (m)	Network	Start	End	In Park?
Calvert Creek	45.883	-113.333	1960	NRCS-SC	1/1/1970	Present	NO
East Fork R.S.	45.917	-113.717	1646	NRCS-SC	1/1/1937	Present	NO
Foolhen	45.750	-113.183	2524	NRCS-SC	1/1/1963	Present	NO
Gibbons Pass	45.700	-113.950	2164	NRCS-SC	1/1/1935	Present	NO
Mudd Lake	45.917	-113.417	2332	NRCS-SC	1/1/1968	Present	NO
Palisade Creek	45.950	-113.467	2515	NRCS-SC	1/1/1967	Present	NO
Saddle Mountain	45.700	-113.967	2420	NRCS-SC	1/1/1965	Present	NO
Slag-A-Melt Lake	45.367	-113.717	2667	NRCS-SC	1/1/1968	Present	NO
Goris Gulch	45.783	-113.350	1917	RAWS	10/1/1987	7/31/1997	NO
Kriley Creek	45.356	-113.893	1585	RAWS	7/1/1990	Present	NO
Sula	45.818	-113.953	1393	RAWS	12/1/2004	Present	NO
Tepee Point	45.935	-113.738	2021	RAWS	2/1/2001	Present	NO
Calvert Creek	45.883	-113.333	1960	SNOTEL	10/1/1975	Present	NO
Moose Creek	45.667	-113.950	1890	SNOTEL	10/1/1981	Present	NO
Saddle Mtn.	45.700	-113.967	2408	SNOTEL	M	M	NO

4.2.2. Lake Roosevelt National Recreation Area

Of the five stations we have identified within the boundaries of LARO, only one is currently active. The RAWS site "Spring Canyon" is located within LARO, about 4 km southeast of the Grand Coulee Dam (Figure 4.2), and has been providing near-real-time data since 1994 (Table 4.4).

There are 17 active COOP stations within 40 km of the boundaries of LARO. "Coulee Dam 1 SW" is the closest active COOP station at the south end of LARO. This station has been operating since 1934 and has a data record that is quite reliable; the last data gaps were one-month gaps that occurred in May, 1992 and January, 1997. "Northport" is the closest active COOP station at the north end of LARO, 10 km up the Columbia River from the northern boundary of LARO. This station has been operating since 1899 and has a reliable data record. The COOP station with the longest data record within 40 km of LARO is "Spokane Intl. Arpt.," which has been active since 1881. This station is about 30 km southeast of the Spokane River arm of LARO. Other long climate records within 40 km of LARO are found at "Wilbur" (1892-present), "Davenport" (1893-present), and "Colville Basic" (1899-present). "Wilbur" and "Davenport" are both 20-30 km south or southeast of LARO and their data records are quite reliable. On the other hand, the data record at "Colville Basic" has significant data gaps, including one gap lasting from 1952 to 1992 and a more recent data gap from October, 2003 to July, 2004.

Twelve active RAWS stations have been identified within 40 km of LARO (Table 4.4) and provide near-real-time data for the region. Many of these stations have been operating since the 1980s. Most of the RAWS stations are located 5-20 km away from the boundaries of LARO. The exception to this pattern is the RAWS station "Kettle Falls," located along the east boundary of LARO in Kettle Falls, Washington (Figure 4.2).

31

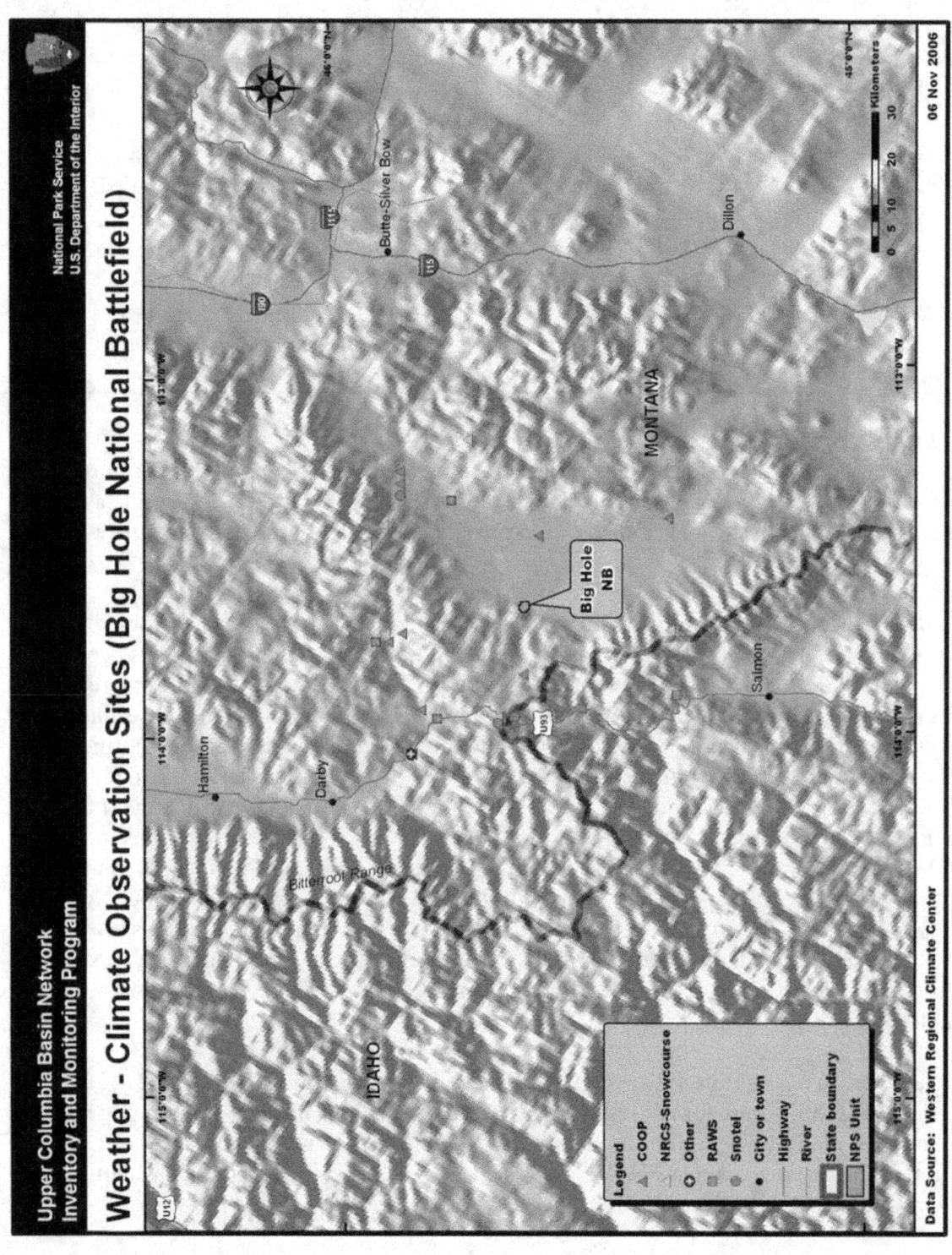

Figure 4.1. Station locations for BIHO.

32

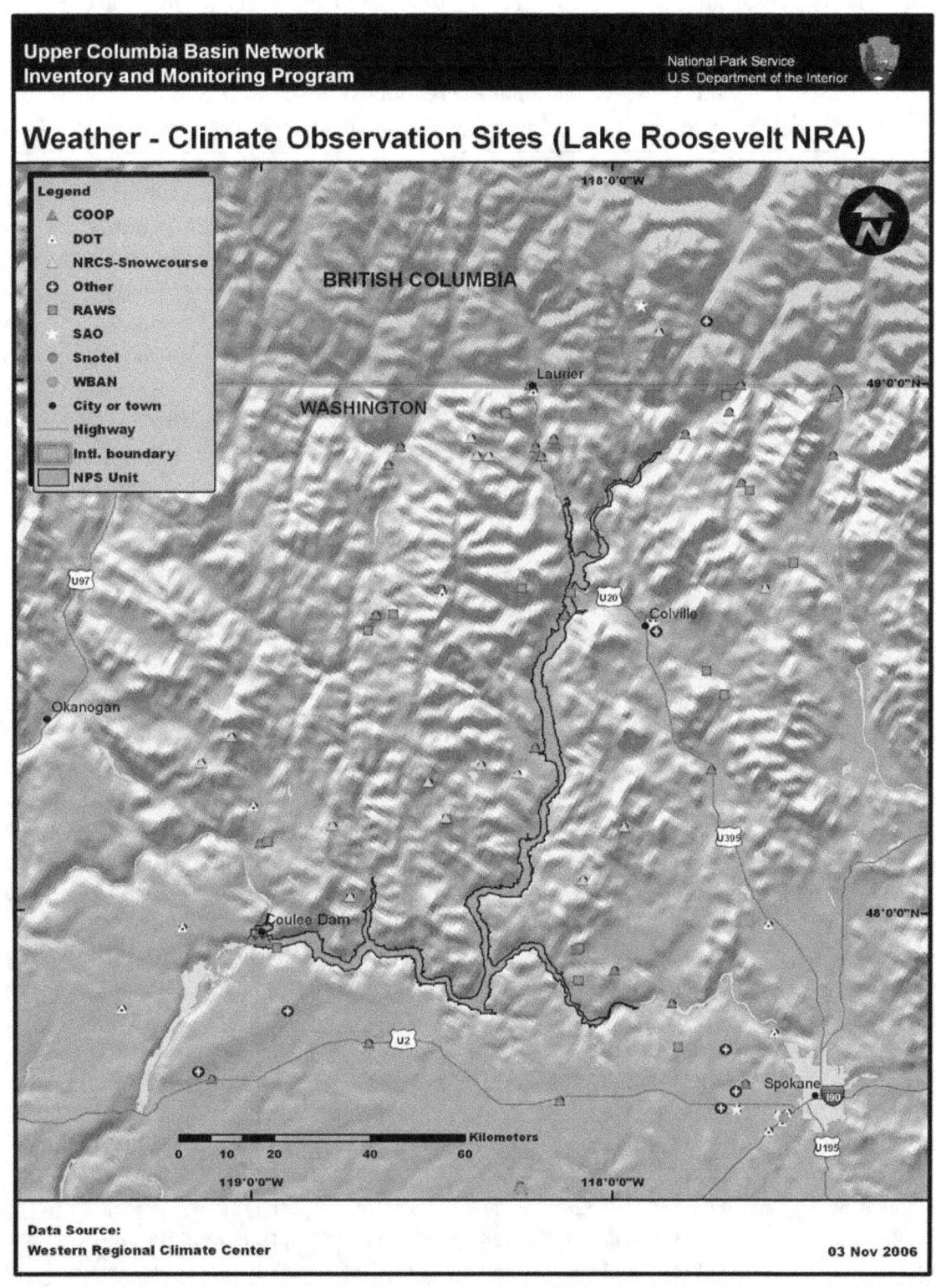

Figure 4.2. Station locations for LARO.

Table 4.4. Weather/climate stations for LARO. Stations inside LARO and within 40 km of the LARO boundary are included. Missing entries are indicated by "M".

Lake Roosevelt National Recreation Area – LARO

Name	Lat.	Lon.	Elev. (m)	Network	Start	End	In Park?
Coulee Dam 1 NE	47.967	-118.983	336	COOP	1/1/1934	12/31/1946	YES
Grand Coulee Dam	47.950	-118.983	393	COOP	6/1/1948	5/31/1967	YES
Grand Coulee Dam 1 N	47.950	-118.967	336	COOP	9/1/1934	4/30/1946	YES
Kettle Falls	48.567	-118.133	387	COOP	2/22/1909	12/31/1939	YES
Spring Canyon	47.935	-118.935	408	RAWS	4/1/1994	Present	YES
Warfield RCS	49.120	-117.730	567	CANADA	M	Present	NO
Boundary	49.000	-117.633	424	COOP	2/1/1945	4/30/1959	NO
Boundary Dam	48.991	-117.359	549	COOP	6/1/1965	Present	NO
Boundary Dam 1 W	48.983	-117.350	793	COOP	11/1/1970	3/12/1973	NO
Boundary Switchyard	48.977	-117.364	762	COOP	7/1/1969	Present	NO
Chewelah	48.275	-117.720	509	COOP	9/1/1925	Present	NO
Colville Airport	48.550	-117.883	575	COOP	11/1/1936	3/15/1988	NO
Colville Basic	48.550	-117.900	505	COOP	9/1/1899	Present	NO
Coulee Dam 1 SW	47.951	-119.005	518	COOP	8/1/1934	Present	NO
Curlew R.S.	48.883	-118.600	564	COOP	7/1/1956	Present	NO
Davenport	47.650	-118.146	744	COOP	3/1/1893	Present	NO
First Thot Lookout	48.900	-118.167	1208	COOP	7/1/1953	Present	NO
Franson Lookout	48.850	-118.633	1156	COOP	7/1/1956	Present	NO
Harrington 1 N	47.483	-118.250	665	COOP	6/1/1948	3/31/1956	NO
Harrington 1 NW	47.490	-118.255	668	COOP	11/1/1961	Present	NO
Hartline	47.686	-119.111	582	COOP	2/1/1927	6/1/2005	NO
Inchelium 2 NW	48.317	-118.217	515	COOP	1/1/1940	10/1/1975	NO
Laurier	49.000	-118.233	501	COOP	4/1/1910	11/17/1986	NO
Long Lake	47.833	-117.833	397	COOP	7/1/1948	2/7/1985	NO
Metaline Falls	48.867	-117.367	644	COOP	12/1/1909	6/18/1965	NO
Nespelem 2 S	48.133	-118.983	576	COOP	2/14/1915	7/1/1991	NO
Northport	48.908	-117.794	411	COOP	4/1/1899	Present	NO
Northport 6 ENE	48.950	-117.667	412	COOP	4/1/1959	4/7/1961	NO
Orient	48.867	-118.200	0	COOP	4/1/1952	3/31/1954	NO
Orient R.S.	48.883	-118.217	485	COOP	6/1/1953	Present	NO
Quartz Lookout	48.567	-118.667	1464	COOP	7/1/1953	Present	NO
Sherman Creek Pass	48.617	-118.483	1699	COOP	10/1/1965	9/30/1976	NO
Spirit	48.817	-117.633	610	COOP	7/1/1958	12/31/1972	NO
Spokane Intl. Arpt.	47.622	-117.528	717	COOP	2/1/1881	Present	NO
Spokane WFO	47.681	-117.627	728	COOP	7/1/1996	Present	NO
Wellpinit	47.896	-117.993	759	COOP	8/1/1923	Present	NO
Wilbur	47.757	-118.678	680	COOP	3/1/1892	Present	NO
CW1001 Almira	47.816	-118.903	769	CWOP	M	Present	NO
CW1101 Hartline	47.700	-119.149	655	CWOP	M	Present	NO

Lake Roosevelt National Recreation Area – LARO

Name	Lat.	Lon.	Elev. (m)	Network	Start	End	In Park?
K7GPS-15 Medical Lake	47.667	-117.654	732	CWOP	M	Present	NO
N7DRK-4 Colville	48.536	-117.876	580	CWOP	M	Present	NO
N7YIM Mt. Vernon	47.746	-117.682	714	CWOP	M	Present	NO
WA7RVV Medical Lake	47.636	-117.696	747	CWOP	M	Present	NO
Baird #2	48.617	-117.567	981	NRCS-SC	1/1/1994	Present	NO
Butte Creek	48.867	-118.383	1241	NRCS-SC	1/1/1961	Present	NO
Disautel Pass	48.283	-119.150	1009	NRCS-SC	M	M	NO
Goat Creek	48.867	-118.350	1097	NRCS-SC	1/1/1961	Present	NO
Gold Mtn. Lookout	48.183	-118.467	1417	NRCS-SC	M	M	NO
Keller Ridge (Disc)	48.167	-118.783	1128	NRCS-SC	1/1/1986	Present	NO
Meteor	48.283	-118.367	677	NRCS-SC	M	M	NO
Moses Mtn. #1	48.333	-119.067	1463	NRCS-SC	1/1/1989	Present	NO
Mount Tolman	48.033	-118.733	732	NRCS-SC	1/1/1985	Present	NO
Record Mountain	49.100	-117.867	-3048	NRCS-SC	M	M	NO
Stranger Mountain	48.167	-117.967	1289	NRCS-SC	1/1/1970	Present	NO
Summit G.S.	48.900	-118.400	1402	NRCS-SC	1/1/1961	Present	NO
Summit G.S. #2	48.900	-118.400	1402	NRCS-SC	1/1/1987	Present	NO
Summit Trail	48.250	-118.517	1170	NRCS-SC	1/1/1986	Present	NO
Togo	48.067	-118.083	1027	NRCS-SC	1/1/1962	Present	NO
Twin Lakes	48.267	-118.267	677	NRCS-SC	1/1/1985	Present	NO
Brown Mtn. Orchard	48.535	-118.689	991	RAWS	10/1/1993	Present	NO
Cedar Creek	48.980	-117.675	1326	RAWS	10/1/1995	8/31/2005	NO
Cliff Ridge	48.417	-117.683	1181	RAWS	6/1/1985	10/31/1993	NO
Deer Mountain	48.802	-117.610	1006	RAWS	1/1/1985	Present	NO
Fry	47.750	-117.817	1280	RAWS	1/1/1985	5/31/1990	NO
Gold Mountain	48.181	-118.464	1428	RAWS	4/1/1991	Present	NO
Iron Mountain	48.567	-118.617	1318	RAWS	1/1/1985	Present	NO
Kettle Falls	48.608	-118.119	399	RAWS	7/1/1995	Present	NO
Lane Creek	48.617	-118.256	1372	RAWS	1/1/1985	Present	NO
Little Pend NWR	48.461	-117.733	614	RAWS	7/1/2000	Present	NO
Midnite 2	47.934	-118.101	762	RAWS	6/1/1998	8/31/2001	NO
Midnite Mine	47.938	-118.094	821	RAWS	4/1/1991	Present	NO
Nespelem	48.136	-118.963	579	RAWS	4/1/1991	Present	NO
Owl Mountain (East)	48.947	-118.302	1073	RAWS	1/1/1985	Present	NO
Teepee Seed Orchard	48.664	-117.482	1024	RAWS	8/1/1995	Present	NO
Wellpinit	47.876	-118.096	683	RAWS	6/1/2002	Present	NO
Colville Airport	48.550	-117.883	575	SAO	11/1/1936	3/15/1988	NO
Colville Basic	48.550	-117.900	505	SAO	9/1/1899	Present	NO
Fairchild AFB	47.633	-117.650	743	SAO	4/1/1940	Present	NO
Old Glory Mountain	49.150	-117.917	2347	SAO	9/1/1944	4/30/1968	NO
Spokane International AP	47.622	-117.528	717	SAO	2/1/1881	Present	NO
Clayton Rd	47.982	-117.560	670	WA DOT	M	Present	NO

Lake Roosevelt National Recreation Area – LARO

Name	Lat.	Lon.	Elev. (m)	Network	Start	End	In Park?
Coulee Dam West	47.972	-119.197	781	WA DOT	M	Present	NO
Laurier	48.989	-118.223	500	WA DOT	M	Present	NO
Mansfield	47.816	-119.363	658	WA DOT	M	Present	NO
Medical Lake at 272	47.592	-117.562	729	WA DOT	M	Present	NO
Nespelem	48.202	-119.004	594	WA DOT	M	Present	NO
Sherman Pass	48.608	-118.479	1676	WA DOT	M	Present	NO
Spokane Intl. AP	47.625	-117.535	609	WA DOT	M	Present	NO
SR 291 Nine Mile	47.777	-117.544	0	WA DOT	M	Present	NO
SR 902 Interchange	47.610	-117.521	725	WA DOT	M	Present	NO
Waste-Energy Plant	47.627	-117.507	0	WA DOT	M	Present	NO
Geiger Field AAF	47.617	-117.517	723	WBAN	8/1/1941	4/30/1963	NO
Harrington	47.483	-118.250	664	WBAN	3/1/1935	11/30/1955	NO

In addition to the 12 RAWS stations near LARO, near-real-time weather data are provided by CWOP, SAO, and WA DOT stations. There are three active SAO stations within 40 km of LARO. Two of these stations are located near Spokane, about 40 km southeast of LARO, while the third SAO station is in Colville, about 20 km east of LARO. These stations each have long records, with the longest record provided by "Spokane Intl. Arpt." (1881-present).

4.2.3. Eastern Oregon/Washington and Northern Idaho

There are two stations located within the boundaries of JODA (Table 4.5), which is broken up into three units. Both are located within the Sheep Rock Unit of JODA, about 50 km west of John Day, Oregon (Figure 4.3). The COOP station "Dayville 8 NW" has been active since 1978. Unfortunately, there are generally no weekend observations each year during the months from November to March. The data record at "Dayville 8 NW" also has several one-month data gaps. These gaps occurred in January, April, and August of 1991; June, 1995; June, 1999; and April and November of 2003. The second COOP station inside JODA, "John Day 35 WNW," started operating in 2004.

In addition to these two stations, we have identified 12 active COOP stations located within 40 km of JODA park unit boundaries (Figure 4.3; Table 4.5). The longest record from among these COOP stations is provided at "Condon," a station located 40 km northeast of the Clarno Unit. This station has been operating since 1894 and has a very complete data record with the exception of a two-month data gap in December, 1996 and January, 1997. The COOP station "Fossil" is about 20 km northeast of the Clarno Unit and just over 40 km north of the Painted Hills Unit. It has been operating since 1923. Numerous data gaps have occurred at this site, particularly in the last 10 years. "Antelope 6 SSW" is located about 40 km southwest of the Clarno Unit of JODA and has been operating since 1924. The COOP station "Ashwood 2 NE" has been active since 1945 and is located 30 km southwest of the Clarno Unit and 40 km northwest of the Painted Hills Unit. This station only measures precipitation.

Table 4.5. Weather/climate stations for UCBN park units in eastern Washington/Oregon and northern Idaho. Stations inside park units and within 40 km of park unit boundaries are included. Missing entries are indicated by "M".

Name	Lat.	Lon.	Elev. (m)	Network	Start	End	In Park?
John Day Fossil Beds National Monument – JODA							
Dayville 8 NW	44.556	-119.645	689	COOP	10/1/1978	Present	YES
John Day 35 WNW	44.556	-119.646	684	COOP	3/19/2004	Present	YES
Antelope 6 SSW	44.820	-120.753	924	COOP	9/1/1924	Present	NO
Ashwood 2 NE	44.750	-120.717	860	COOP	10/1/1945	Present	NO
Beech Creek	44.567	-119.117	1437	COOP	8/1/1909	5/31/1949	NO
Buckhorn Ranch	45.083	-120.450	915	COOP	7/26/1966	10/1/1976	NO
Condon	45.233	-120.181	866	COOP	7/23/1894	Present	NO
Dayville	44.467	-119.533	720	COOP	6/1/1895	10/11/1978	NO
Derr Guard Stn.	44.450	-119.933	1769	COOP	9/1/1963	10/31/1976	NO
Fossil	44.999	-120.211	808	COOP	7/1/1923	Present	NO
Fox	44.650	-119.150	1339	COOP	5/1/1949	7/31/1957	NO
Hay Creek	44.950	-120.900	897	COOP	10/1/1909	12/31/1945	NO
Ingram Spring	44.550	-120.517	1525	COOP	6/1/1967	10/31/1976	NO
Kent	45.197	-120.699	826	COOP	12/22/1922	3/22/2005	NO
Kinzua	45.033	-119.917	1052	COOP	7/1/1930	12/31/1943	NO
Kinzua Pine Mills	44.967	-119.917	1269	COOP	6/1/1953	Present	NO
Marks Creek Guard Stn.	44.500	-120.383	1403	COOP	12/1/1960	10/31/1976	NO
Mitchell 2	44.567	-120.150	903	COOP	6/1/1962	6/22/1965	NO
Mitchell 2 E	44.568	-120.116	1012	COOP	5/8/1996	Present	NO
Mitchell 2 NW	44.583	-120.183	806	COOP	12/1/1906	3/1/1994	NO
Monument	44.815	-119.431	597	COOP	4/1/1967	Present	NO
Monument 2	44.819	-119.420	608	COOP	2/1/1961	Present	NO
Monument R.S.	44.818	-119.421	604	COOP	10/1/1915	Present	NO
Ochoco R.S.	44.396	-120.426	1212	COOP	7/1/1948	Present	NO
Pisgah Lookout	44.450	-120.250	2044	COOP	7/1/1953	Present	NO
Rager R.S.	44.233	-119.733	1220	COOP	7/1/1953	3/20/1975	NO
Snow Board Ridge	44.967	-119.983	1559	COOP	7/1/1966	10/31/1976	NO
Spray	44.819	-119.776	545	COOP	1/1/1937	Present	NO
CW2286 Monument	44.821	-119.419	616	CWOP	M	Present	NO
CW3255 Dayville	44.466	-119.540	744	CWOP	M	Present	NO
CW4012 Mitchell	44.564	-120.147	891	CWOP	M	Present	NO
N7GSU Fossil	44.996	-120.212	814	CWOP	M	Present	NO
Derr	44.450	-119.933	1728	NRCS-SC	1/1/1937	Present	NO
Marks Creek	44.483	-120.400	1384	NRCS-SC	1/1/1938	Present	NO
Ochoco Meadows	44.433	-120.333	1585	NRCS-SC	1/1/1928	Present	NO
Cow Canyon (US 97 MP 68.9)	44.894	-120.937	948	ODOT	M	Present	NO
Kent (US 97 MP 40.9)	45.194	-120.696	824	ODOT	M	Present	NO
Keys Butte (HWY 41 MP	44.552	-120.044	1333	ODOT	M	Present	NO

Name	Lat.	Lon.	Elev. (m)	Network	Start	End	In Park?
74)							
Mount Identifier US 97 MP 61	44.990	-120.849	1061	ODOT	M	Present	NO
Shaniko (US 97 MP 56)	45.003	-120.753	1018	ODOT	M	Present	NO
Arlington 8 ENE	44.741	-120.030	107	PDTWFO	M	Present	NO
Condon	45.232	-120.182	860	PDTWFO	M	Present	NO
Kent	45.190	-120.690	826	PDTWFO	M	Present	NO
Keyes Summit	44.550	-120.040	1333	PDTWFO	M	Present	NO
Shaniko	45.000	-120.750	1018	PDTWFO	M	Present	NO
Spray	44.840	-119.790	545	PDTWFO	M	Present	NO
Winlock	44.912	-119.892	960	PDTWFO	M	Present	NO
Board Creek	44.593	-119.278	1524	RAWS	10/1/1986	Present	NO
Board Hollow	44.606	-120.683	1256	RAWS	10/1/1986	Present	NO
Briar Rabbit	44.323	-119.767	1798	RAWS	5/1/1993	Present	NO
Cold Springs	44.350	-120.130	1431	RAWS	1/1/1985	Present	NO
Meyers Canyon	44.610	-120.182	890	RAWS	5/1/1989	4/30/1997	NO
Mitchell	44.582	-120.179	799	RAWS	2/1/2003	Present	NO
North Pole Ridge	45.038	-120.531	1061	RAWS	8/1/1990	Present	NO
Slide Mountain	44.463	-120.294	1737	RAWS	5/1/1985	Present	NO
Derr.	44.450	-119.933	1728	SNOTEL	10/1/1980	Present	NO
Ochoco Meadows	44.433	-120.333	1585	SNOTEL	10/1/1980	Present	NO
Condon	45.250	-120.183	887	WBAN	10/1/1943	9/30/1945	NO
Nez Perce National Historical Park – NEPE							
Spalding	46.450	-116.817	235	COOP	8/1/1948	12/31/1978	YES
Imbler	45.433	-117.967	838	Agrimet	6/1/2001	12/31/2001	NO
Adams R.S.	45.650	-116.033	1586	COOP	6/1/1953	12/31/1958	NO
Ahsahka	46.517	-116.300	0	COOP	8/1/1948	10/31/1965	NO
Alpowa Ranch	46.417	-117.200	232	COOP	7/1/1927	12/31/1936	NO
Anatone	46.133	-117.133	1098	COOP	8/31/1912	12/1/1981	NO
Anatone Telemark	46.100	-116.983	246	COOP	9/1/1959	5/1/1998	NO
Aneroid Lake	45.217	-117.200	2257	COOP	8/1/1963	10/31/1976	NO
Asotin 14 SW	46.201	-117.252	1067	COOP	6/1/1976	Present	NO
Asotin 4 SW George C	46.300	-117.117	332	COOP	8/1/1976	7/13/1992	NO
Asotin 5 WSW	46.333	-117.150	332	COOP	1/1/1976	1/15/1983	NO
Asotin Asotin Creek	46.333	-117.067	235	COOP	4/1/1976	3/6/1986	NO
Castle Creek R.S.	45.833	-115.967	686	COOP	5/1/1954	Present	NO
Chinook	48.588	-109.226	738	COOP	11/1/1895	Present	NO
Chinook 35 SE	48.173	-109.004	1024	COOP	6/1/2001	Present	NO
Clarkston Heights	46.383	-117.083	363	COOP	11/1/1937	1/31/1960	NO
Cleveland	48.267	-109.150	1068	COOP	2/17/1903	6/30/1957	NO
Cleveland 5 ENE	48.317	-109.067	1016	COOP	6/1/1957	12/1/1989	NO
Cold Springs Lookout	45.500	-116.450	2111	COOP	7/1/1953	Present	NO
Coolwater Lookout	46.150	-115.450	2114	COOP	8/1/1915	Present	NO

Name	Lat.	Lon.	Elev. (m)	Network	Start	End	In Park?
Cornucopia	45.000	-117.200	1434	COOP	7/1/1909	8/29/1974	NO
Cottonwood	46.017	-116.333	1040	COOP	4/1/1893	8/19/1976	NO
Cottonwood 2 WSW	46.034	-116.392	1202	COOP	2/3/1950	Present	NO
Cove	45.300	-117.800	890	COOP	10/10/1973	8/5/1988	NO
Cove 1 E	45.296	-117.790	954	COOP	3/1/1917	Present	NO
Craigmont	46.233	-116.483	1143	COOP	8/1/1948	12/31/1996	NO
Dworshak Fish Hatchery	46.502	-116.322	303	COOP	10/1/1966	Present	NO
Elgin	45.562	-117.920	809	COOP	8/1/1937	6/12/2006	NO
Elk River 1 S	46.774	-116.176	889	COOP	1/1/1952	Present	NO
Enterprise 16 NNE	45.567	-117.083	1321	COOP	6/1/1958	2/28/1963	NO
Enterprise 2 S	45.400	-117.267	1183	COOP	4/1/1963	7/8/1995	NO
Enterprise 20 NNE	45.708	-117.153	1000	COOP	2/1/1969	Present	NO
Enterprise 21 NNE	45.683	-117.100	1074	COOP	2/1/1963	2/12/1969	NO
Enterprise R.S.	45.426	-117.297	1163	COOP	12/1/1931	Present	NO
Fenn R.S.	46.093	-115.536	475	COOP	6/1/1939	Present	NO
Flora 7 SSE	45.800	-117.267	1464	COOP	9/1/1964	10/31/1976	NO
Grangeville	45.929	-116.122	1021	COOP	10/1/1893	Present	NO
Grangeville 1 N	45.940	-116.121	1009	COOP	10/1/1999	Present	NO
Grangeville 11 SE	45.833	-115.933	686	COOP	11/1/1964	Present	NO
Greencreek 3 N	46.150	-116.267	1022	COOP	11/1/1964	3/19/1972	NO
Harl Butte	45.333	-116.883	1678	COOP	7/1/1953	Present	NO
Harlem 4 SSE	48.500	-108.750	708	COOP	4/1/1966	3/10/1987	NO
Harlem 4 W	48.552	-108.859	720	COOP	10/1/1896	Present	NO
Havre	48.567	-109.667	760	COOP	11/20/1879	1/31/1961	NO
Havre 7th Ave Bridge	48.550	-109.667	759	COOP	3/1/1957	3/1/1981	NO
Howardville	45.650	-117.667	1089	COOP	7/1/1948	10/31/1955	NO
Imnaha	45.562	-116.833	600	COOP	7/1/1948	Present	NO
Imnaha 2	45.567	-116.833	604	COOP	2/1/1962	9/13/1965	NO
Joseph	45.346	-117.225	1298	COOP	1/1/1893	Present	NO
Kamiah	46.230	-116.034	375	COOP	1/14/1913	Present	NO
Kooskia	46.150	-115.983	390	COOP	11/16/1908	1/15/1988	NO
Kooskia 5 SSE	46.071	-115.934	710	COOP	3/22/1988	5/1/2006	NO
Laird Creek	45.874	-114.053	1294	COOP	5/15/2001	Present	NO
Lapwai 2 N	46.423	-116.811	264	COOP	3/1/1916	11/10/2005	NO
Lewiston	46.417	-117.033	216	COOP	9/1/1881	7/1/1973	NO
Lewiston Nez Perce Co. Arpt.	46.375	-117.016	438	COOP	10/1/1946	Present	NO
Lewiston No 2	46.375	-116.998	442	COOP	5/1/1998	3/1/2004	NO
Lewiston Water Plant	46.417	-117.017	226	COOP	2/1/1894	12/31/1955	NO
Lloyd	48.300	-109.350	1190	COOP	6/1/1951	7/31/1958	NO
Lostine 4 NE	45.523	-117.374	1152	COOP	2/2/2002	Present	NO
Lowell Lochsa	46.150	-115.583	442	COOP	3/1/1959	4/30/1978	NO
Lowell Selway	46.083	-115.517	470	COOP	3/1/1959	4/30/1978	NO

Name	Lat.	Lon.	Elev. (m)	Network	Start	End	In Park?
Lucile	45.533	-116.300	491	COOP	7/1/1979	10/30/1980	NO
Minam 7 NE	45.683	-117.600	1102	COOP	10/1/1955	8/11/1986	NO
Moscow 5 NE	46.790	-116.920	914	COOP	7/1/1972	Present	NO
Moscow U Of I	46.724	-116.961	811	COOP	11/7/1893	Present	NO
Mount Fanny	45.317	-117.733	2141	COOP	7/1/1965	3/1/1975	NO
Musselshell R.S.	46.367	-115.750	967	COOP	12/1/1913	Present	NO
Nezperce	46.236	-116.247	988	COOP	12/10/1901	Present	NO
Nezperce	46.233	-116.233	939	COOP	8/1/1948	9/30/1951	NO
Ohara Bar	46.083	-115.517	473	COOP	11/1/1909	6/30/1915	NO
Orofino	46.483	-116.267	402	COOP	8/17/1903	1/31/1982	NO
Orofino 3 E	46.473	-116.178	405	COOP	1/22/2004	Present	NO
Orofino Telemark	46.483	-116.267	0	COOP	11/1/1965	4/30/1967	NO
Peck Telemark	46.500	-116.400	0	COOP	10/1/1965	4/30/1967	NO
Pete King R.S.	46.150	-115.600	473	COOP	7/1/1921	12/31/1939	NO
Pierce	46.492	-115.801	939	COOP	6/1/1962	Present	NO
Pierce R.S.	46.500	-115.800	967	COOP	11/1/1913	3/31/1963	NO
Pullman 2 E	46.717	-117.150	769	COOP	11/9/1951	Present	NO
Reubens	46.333	-116.550	1074	COOP	12/1/1979	5/31/1980	NO
Riggins	45.424	-116.315	549	COOP	2/1/1896	Present	NO
Slate Creek R.S.	45.633	-116.283	485	COOP	7/1/1957	10/20/1971	NO
Taylor Green	45.083	-117.550	1769	COOP	9/1/1964	10/31/1976	NO
Tope Lookout	45.667	-117.400	1281	COOP	7/1/1953	Present	NO
Walde Mountain	46.250	-115.633	1525	COOP	10/1/1965	9/30/1976	NO
Wallowa	45.572	-117.531	891	COOP	3/1/1903	Present	NO
Wallowa R.S.	45.583	-117.533	897	COOP	7/1/1953	Present	NO
White Bird	45.750	-116.323	431	COOP	12/1/1913	10/10/2005	NO
Winchester	46.238	-116.623	1204	COOP	6/17/1965	Present	NO
Winchester 1 SE	46.233	-116.617	1205	COOP	8/1/1939	6/17/1965	NO
CW1102 Wallowa	45.570	-117.530	898	CWOP	M	Present	NO
CW1430 Enterprise	45.427	-117.292	1177	CWOP	M	Present	NO
CW1621 Reubens	46.354	-116.532	1061	CWOP	M	Present	NO
CW2049 Imnaha	45.560	-116.835	603	CWOP	M	Present	NO
CW2874 Havre	48.557	-109.638	789	CWOP	M	Present	NO
CW2920 Helix	45.850	-118.654	535	CWOP	M	Present	NO
CW3808 Enterprise	45.426	-117.268	1197	CWOP	M	Present	NO
CW5857 Clarkston	46.415	-117.042	245	CWOP	M	Present	NO
KB7DZR Joseph	45.390	-117.238	1214	CWOP	M	Present	NO
KC7PHC Orofino	46.473	-116.247	408	CWOP	M	Present	NO
Paradise Ridge	46.677	-116.994	896	ITD	M	Present	NO
Reisenauer Hill	46.653	-117.000	896	ITD	M	Present	NO
Snow Road	46.677	-117.050	768	ITD	M	Present	NO
Winchester	46.255	-116.605	1209	ITD	M	Present	NO
Riggins	45.490	-116.330	537	KBCI	M	Present	NO

Name	Lat.	Lon.	Elev. (m)	Network	Start	End	In Park?
Bullhook	48.419	-109.616	987	MCSCN	M	Present	NO
Grangeville 1N	45.940	-116.120	1009	MSOWFO	M	Present	NO
Orofino School	46.480	-116.240	325	MSOWFO	M	Present	NO
Bald Mtn. AM OR	45.217	-117.650	2042	NRCS-SC	1/1/1960	Present	NO
Big Sheep AM	45.167	-117.083	1890	NRCS-SC	1/1/1963	Present	NO
Boxelder Creek	48.167	-109.600	1554	NRCS-SC	1/1/1975	Present	NO
East Eagle	45.033	-117.317	1341	NRCS-SC	1/1/1991	Present	NO
Mirror Lake AM	45.167	-117.300	2499	NRCS-SC	1/1/1963	Present	NO
Pierce R.S.	46.500	-115.800	939	NRCS-SC	1/1/1951	Present	NO
Rocky Boy	48.183	-109.650	1433	NRCS-SC	1/1/1941	Present	NO
Standley AM	45.550	-117.567	2256	NRCS-SC	1/1/1961	Present	NO
Sucker Creek	48.283	-109.617	1207	NRCS-SC	1/1/1973	Present	NO
Taylor Road	48.267	-109.700	1244	NRCS-SC	1/1/1973	Present	NO
TV Ridge AM	45.400	-117.383	1728	NRCS-SC	1/1/1965	Present	NO
Webb Creek	46.150	-116.767	1439	NRCS-SC	1/1/1979	Present	NO
West Eagle Meadows AM	45.083	-117.483	1676	NRCS-SC	1/1/1976	Present	NO
Bobcat Creek	45.848	-117.384	1280	RAWS	4/1/1988	10/31/1998	NO
Cotton	46.023	-116.883	893	RAWS	2/1/2002	Present	NO
Craig Mountain (Portable)	46.128	-116.818	1426	RAWS	5/1/1998	10/31/1998	NO
Dent	46.622	-116.218	518	RAWS	5/1/1998	Present	NO
Eden	45.927	-117.588	1280	RAWS	5/1/1990	Present	NO
Fenn	46.100	-115.535	463	RAWS	6/1/1996	Present	NO
Fort Belknap	48.304	-108.719	812	RAWS	7/1/1992	Present	NO
Grangeville	45.938	-116.123	1005	RAWS	6/1/1993	7/31/1994	NO
Harl Butte	45.319	-116.868	1850	RAWS	7/1/1991	Present	NO
Kuhn Ridge	45.758	-117.353	1402	RAWS	8/1/1985	11/30/1987	NO
LaGrande 1	45.553	-118.012	945	RAWS	6/1/1997	Present	NO
Lapwai	46.394	-116.801	311	RAWS	8/1/1998	7/31/1999	NO
Miller Butte	45.233	-116.950	1737	RAWS	6/1/1988	11/30/1988	NO
Minam Lodge-Portable	45.354	-117.633	1090	RAWS	8/1/1995	Present	NO
Nez Perce Tribe-Spaulding	46.448	-116.825	228	RAWS	7/1/2004	Present	NO
Pierce	46.500	-115.833	940	RAWS	4/1/1990	Present	NO
Pittsburg Landing	45.638	-116.469	351	RAWS	10/1/1993	Present	NO
Point Prom II	45.355	-117.704	2014	RAWS	7/1/2000	Present	NO
Point Prominence	45.372	-117.702	2060	RAWS	1/1/1992	7/31/2000	NO
Roberts Butte	45.682	-117.206	1299	RAWS	10/1/1998	Present	NO
Rudo	46.502	-115.993	727	RAWS	10/1/2003	Present	NO
Shell	46.367	-115.833	975	RAWS	5/1/1985	11/30/1989	NO
Slate Creek Idaho	45.633	-116.283	478	RAWS	5/1/1998	Present	NO
Grangeville	45.929	-116.122	1021	SAO	10/1/1893	Present	NO
Kamiah	46.230	-116.034	375	SAO	1/14/1913	Present	NO
Lewiston Nez Perce Co. Arpt.	46.375	-117.016	438	SAO	10/1/1946	Present	NO

Name	Lat.	Lon.	Elev. (m)	Network	Start	End	In Park?
Lowell Three Rivers Resort	46.144	-115.596	451	SAO	8/23/1982	Present	NO
Pullman Moscow Reg. Arpt.	46.744	-117.109	778	SAO	6/1/1947	Present	NO
Aneroid Lake #2	45.217	-117.200	2225	SNOTEL	10/1/1980	Present	NO
Moss Springs	45.267	-117.683	1783	SNOTEL	10/1/1980	Present	NO
Mt. Howard	45.267	-117.167	2411	SNOTEL	10/1/1980	Present	NO
Rocky Boy	48.183	-109.650	1433	SNOTEL	M	M	NO
Schneider Meadows	45.000	-117.150	1646	SNOTEL	10/1/1980	Present	NO
Uniontown	46.517	-117.081	815	WA DOT	M	Present	NO
Whitman Mission National Historic Site – WHMI							
Dixie 4 SE	46.091	-118.101	686	COOP	6/1/1948	Present	NO
Garden City Heights	46.083	-118.317	320	COOP	5/16/1916	12/31/1942	NO
Gibbon	45.700	-118.367	530	COOP	2/1/1964	3/1/1996	NO
Gibbon 3 NE	45.720	-118.322	565	COOP	4/12/1966	Present	NO
Ice Harbor Dam	46.245	-118.879	112	COOP	3/1/1957	Present	NO
Mill Creek	46.017	-118.117	610	COOP	10/1/1915	10/1/1973	NO
Mill Creek Dam	46.076	-118.274	358	COOP	6/1/1948	Present	NO
Milton 5 SE	45.883	-118.283	400	COOP	7/1/1948	8/31/1951	NO
Milton Freewater	45.943	-118.409	296	COOP	1/1/1928	Present	NO
Pendleton Br Exp. Stn.	45.721	-118.626	453	COOP	1/1/1932	Present	NO
Tollgate 2	45.783	-118.117	1531	COOP	10/1/1962	1/24/1964	NO
Touchet	46.033	-118.667	134	COOP	2/21/1905	12/31/1940	NO
Touchet Ridge	46.117	-117.983	1098	COOP	3/1/1909	12/31/1943	NO
Walla Walla 13 ESE	45.992	-118.051	732	COOP	2/10/1948	Present	NO
Walla Walla 14 ENE	46.100	-118.167	1086	COOP	2/1/1972	11/9/1972	NO
Walla Walla 15 ESE	46.017	-118.017	1336	COOP	M	6/30/1965	NO
Walla Walla 3 W	46.050	-118.400	244	COOP	1/1/1931	9/29/1962	NO
Walla Walla City	46.065	-118.313	315	COOP	12/10/2001	Present	NO
Walla Walla Reg. Arpt.	46.095	-118.287	355	COOP	7/1/1930	Present	NO
Walla Walla WSO	46.033	-118.333	289	COOP	11/1/1893	Present	NO
Weston	45.821	-118.430	586	COOP	3/1/1953	Present	NO
Weston 2 SE	45.800	-118.400	641	COOP	2/1/1893	3/31/1955	NO
Weston 5 ESE	45.800	-118.333	976	COOP	3/1/1955	11/1/1982	NO
Whitman Mission	46.044	-118.463	193	COOP	9/30/1962	Present	YES
CW0682 Helix	45.892	-118.657	578	CWOP	M	Present	NO
CW0706 Athena	45.812	-118.422	584	CWOP	M	Present	NO
CW1144 Walla Walla	46.049	-118.299	337	CWOP	M	Present	NO
CW2313 Tollgate	45.786	-118.109	1547	CWOP	M	Present	NO
CW2748 Walla Walla	46.056	-118.359	270	CWOP	M	Present	NO
CW2850 Walla Walla	46.068	-118.304	324	CWOP	M	Present	NO
CW2920 Helix	45.850	-118.654	535	CWOP	M	Present	NO
KE7FQA Walla Walla	46.041	-118.221	419	CWOP	M	Present	NO
Tollgate	45.833	-118.133	1545	NRCS-SC	1/1/1931	Present	NO

Name	Lat.	Lon.	Elev. (m)	Network	Start	End	In Park?
Walla Walla-Whitman College	46.070	-118.330	323	PDTWFO	M	Present	NO
Walla Walla Reg. Arpt.	46.095	-118.287	355	SAO	7/1/1930	Present	NO
Walla Walla AAF	46.100	-118.283	368	WBAN	9/1/1941	12/31/1951	NO

The COOP station "Mitchell 2 E" is only 10 km east of the Painted Hills Unit of JODA (Figure 4.3) and is the closest active COOP station to this unit. This station has been active since 1996 (Table 4.5). The COOP station "Pisgah Lookout" is 20 km south of the Painted Hills Unit of JODA and has been active since 1953. The COOP station "Ochoco R.S." is 30 km southwest of the Painted Hills Unit of JODA and has been active since 1948.

The Sheep Rock Unit of JODA has several active COOPs located within 40 km of the unit. "Monument R.S.," located 30 km northeast of the Sheep Rock Unit, has been operating since 1915, but the data are of uncertain quality. Two other COOP stations in the Monument area ("Monument" and "Monument 2") have also been active since the 1960s. The data records at these sites are largely complete, although there have been no weekend observations at "Monument 2" since about 1989. The COOP station "Spray" is about 30 km northwest of the Sheep Rock Unit and although it has operated since 1937, like "Monument R.S.," the data are of uncertain quality. "Kinzua Pine Mills" is about 40 km northwest of the Sheep Rock Unit and has operated since 1953.

Near-real-time data in the JODA are provided by stations associated with ODOT, PDTWFO, and the RAWS and SNOTEL networks. We have identified seven active RAWS stations within 40 km of JODA park unit boundaries (Figure 4.3; Table 4.5). Most of these stations have been operating since the 1980s. Two RAWS stations are located within 40 km of the Sheep Rock Unit. These include "Board Creek," 20 km to the east, and "Briar Rabbit," 30 km to the southwest. Four RAWS stations are located within 40 km of the Painted Hills Unit. The closest RAWS station, "Mitchell," is 10 km southeast of the unit. Two RAWS station are located between 20-30 km south of the unit (Cold Springs and Slide Mountain). "Board Hollow" is 30 km to the west of this unit. One RAWS station is located about 10 km east of the Clarno Unit (North Pole Ridge).

We have identified two active SNOTEL stations within 40 km of JODA park unit boundaries (Figure 4.3; Table 4.5). Both of these stations have been operating since 1980. "Ochoco Meadows" is located in the Ochoco Mountains, 20 km south of the Painted Hills Unit, while "Derr" is about 30 km away from both the Painted Hills and Sheep Rock Units.

We have identified only one weather/climate station within the various units of NEPE (Table 4.5). This station, "Spalding," is a historical COOP station that operated at the Spalding Visitor Center from 1948 to 1978. However, there are at least 55 active COOP stations within 40 km of NEPE unit boundaries. The COOP station "Lewiston Nez Perce Co. Arpt." is located about 15 km southwest of the Spalding Visitor Center and has a reliable data record that starts in 1946. The COOP station "Moscow U of I" is located about 30 km north of the Spalding Visitor Center and has a data record going back to 1893. This station's data record is very complete, with the exception of a data gap from July, 1925 to March, 1926. There are at least four long-term active

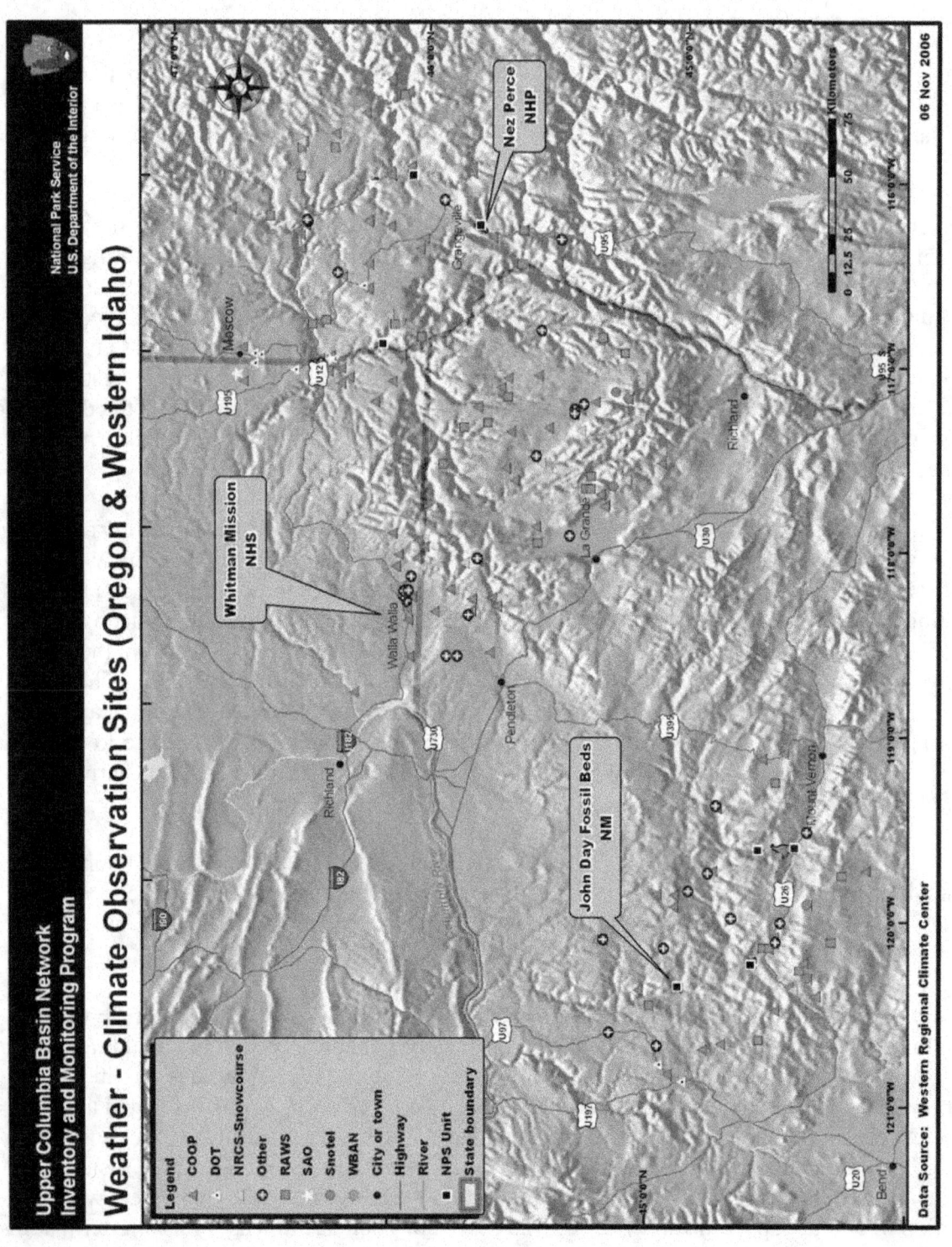

Figure 4.3. Station locations for UCBN park units in eastern Washington/Oregon and northern Idaho.

44

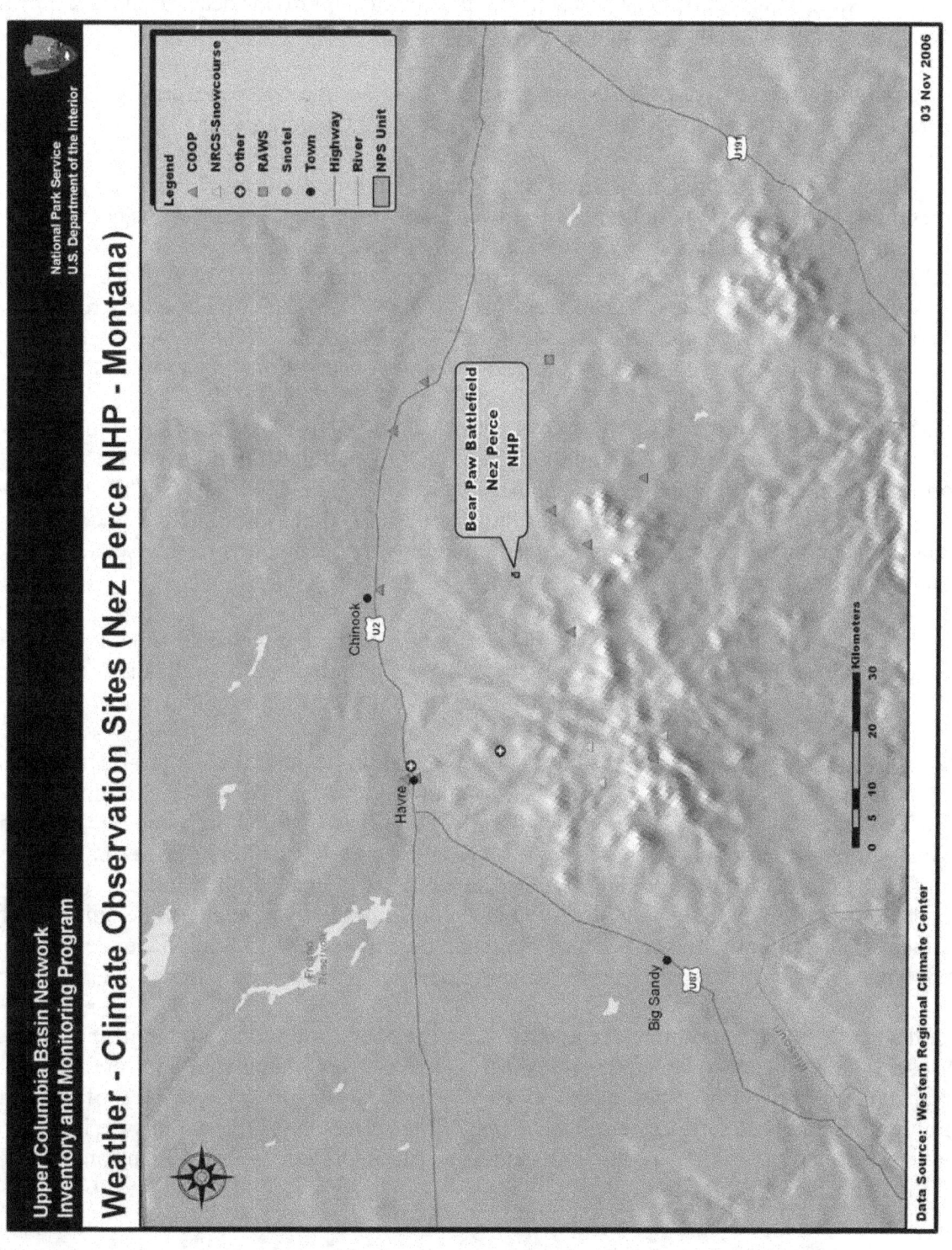

Figure 4.4. Station locations for Bear Paw Battlefield.

45

COOP stations within 40 km of the Heart of the Monster unit of NEPE. The COOP station "Nezperce" is located 20 km west of Heart of the Monster and it has been active since 1901. However, significant data gaps have occurred at this site, most notably from November, 1995 to December, 1996 and in February, 2002. The COOP station "Kamiah" (1913-present) is just east of the Heart of the Monster unit but has unreliable data. Two other long-term COOP stations, "Musselshell R.S." and "Coolwater Lookout," are located 30-40 km northeast of the Heart of the Monster unit and have data records going back to the 1910s.

There are two long-term active COOP stations within 40 km of the Old Chief Joseph Gravesite (Table 4.5). The COOP station "Joseph" is located in Joseph, Oregon, the same town where Old Chief Joseph Gravesite is located, and it has been active since 1893. However, the data from this site are not reliable. A more reliable station is the COOP station "Wallowa," located 40 km northwest of the gravesite. This station has been active since 1903. The station has data gaps from December, 1996 to January, 1997; from June, 1997 to August, 1998; and in April, 2003. The COOP station "Grangeville" is the primary long-term station within 40 km of the White Bird Battlefield unit of NEPE and has been active since 1893. This station has a very reliable data record. A COOP station operated very near the White Bird Battlefield from 1913-2005 (White Bird), but this station appears to have ceased taking observations in October of 2005.

There are two long-term active COOP stations within 40 km of the Bear Paw Battlefield, located in northcentral Montana (Figure 4.4; Table 4.5). The COOP station "Harlem 4 W" is located 30 km northeast of the Bear Paw Battlefield and has been active since 1896. The COOP station "Chinook" is located 20 km north of the Bear Paw Battlefield and has been active since 1895. The data records from both stations are fairly complete, with both stations having scattered data gaps during the 1970s and 1980s.

We have identified numerous automated stations currently providing near-real-time weather data within 40 km of the NEPE units (Figure 4.3-4.4; Table 4.5). Eighteen of these stations are RAWS stations, five of the stations are SAO stations, and at least four are SNOTEL stations.

For the Old Chief Joseph Gravesite, the closest RAWS station we identified is "Harl Butte," about 30 km east of the unit. For the White Bird Battlefield, there are two RAWS stations within 20 km of the unit. "Slate Creek" is 20 km south of this unit, while "Pittsburg Landing" is 20 km southwest of the unit, along the Snake River. The RAWS station "Nez Perce Tribe Spalding" is just outside the grounds of the Spalding Visitor Center. For the Heart of the Monster unit of NEPE, the closest RAWS station we identified is "Fenn," about 30 km south of the unit. Finally, for the Bear Paw Battlefield in northcentral Montana, the closest RAWS station we identified is "Fort Belknap," about 30 km northeast of the unit.

Two of the active SNOTEL stations we identified for the NEPE are within 20 km of the Old Chief Joseph Gravesite. "Mt. Howard" and "Aneroid Lake" are 15 km and 20 km south of this unit, respectively. A SNOTEL station "Rocky Boy" was identified 40 km southwest of the Bear Paw Battlefield, but its status is uncertain. The rest of the active SNOTEL stations we identified are scattered around the Wallowa Mountains in northeastern Oregon, within 40 km south and east of the Old Chief Joseph Gravesite.

Five active SAO stations are located within 40 km of NEPE units (Table 4.5). No SAO stations were identified near Bear Paw Battlefield and the Old Chief Joseph Gravesite. The closest SAO station to the White Bird Battlefield is "Grangeville," which has operated since 1893. The closest SAO station to the Spalding Visitor Center is "Lewiston Nez Perce Co. Arpt.," which has operated since 1946 and is 20 km west of the visitor center. "Kamiah" is the closest SAO station to the Heart of the Monster unit of NEPE, but its data record is of questionable quality.

There is one station located inside WHMI. This is a COOP station (Whitman Mission) that has been active since 1962. The data record at this station is quite complete. In addition, we have identified 11 COOP stations that are active within 40 km of the boundaries of WHMI. The COOP station "Walla Walla WSO" is located just 10 km east of WHMI and has been active since 1893, making it the longest data record of any of the COOP stations we identified around WHMI. The data record at this station was complete until January of 1987, when a significant data gap began and lasted until May of 2001. Weather observations have been sporadic since 2001. More complete long-term data records are obtainable from the COOP stations "Milton-Freewater" (1928-present), located 15 km south of WHMI, and "Pendleton Br. Exp. Stn." (1932-present), located 30 km south of WHMI. An additional long-term record is found at the COOP station "Walla Walla Reg. Arpt.," which is 10 km east of WHMI and has been active since 1930. The data record at this station had a significant data gap from February, 1994 to September, 1996. This site also houses a SAO station that now provides near-real-time data for WHMI. A PDTWFO station and several CWOP stations also provide near-real-time data for WHMI.

4.2.3. Southern Idaho

There are no weather/climate stations located within CIRO (Table 4.6). Three active COOP stations are located within 40 km of CIRO. The station "Oakley," which is almost 40 km northwest of CIRO (Figure 4.5), has the longest record of these active COOP stations, going back to 1893. The data record at "Oakley" is very complete. No data gaps have occurred at this station during the past 25 years.

After "Oakley," the SAO and COOP stations at Malta, Idaho, have the next longest data records, going back to 1952. Malta is about 40 km northeast of CIRO. The data records from these two stations are quite reliable. There are some automated stations that are somewhat closer to CIRO than the SAO station at Malta. These include the RAWS station "Goose Creek" and the SNOTEL station "Howell Canyon". "Goose Creek" is about 30 km west of CIRO (Figure 4.5) and has collected data since 1990 (Table 4.6). "Howell Canyon" is located about 30 km north of CIRO, at the north end of the Albion Mountains, and has collected data since 1980. The SNOTEL station "Bostetter R.S." also provides near-real-time data for the CIRO region; however, it is located 40 km west of CIRO, across the Goose Creek Valley, and is likely not as representative of the CIRO area as are thee automated stations that were previously discussed. Craters of the Moon National Monument and Preserve (CRMO) has at least five stations located inside its boundaries (Figure 4.5), all of which are active (Table 4.6). Two of these stations are COOP stations. The COOP station "Craters of the Moon" has the longest data record of any of the stations within CRMO, going back to 1958. This station has had occasional data gaps lasting one month or longer throughout its history. The last such gap was a one-month gap in April, 1998. An ARL FRD station (Craters of the Moon) is active near the main visitor center in CRMO. Located nearby is a GPMP station (also called "Craters of the Moon") that has been active in CRMO since 1992. Both of these provide near-real-time data. Finally, a RAWS station (Potter Butte) is located about 20 km southeast of the main visitor center and has provided near-real-time data since 1990.

Thirty of the 55 COOP stations we identified within 40 km of the CRMO boundary are active (Table 4.6). The station "Buhl No 2," which is almost 40 km southwest of CIRO (Figure 4.5), has the longest record of these active COOP stations, going back to 1906. However, the data record at "Buhl No 2" has been quite unreliable since 1977. A more reliable long-term record is provided at the COOP station "Shoshone 1 WNW." This station is 30 km west of CRMO and has been active since 1908. Although there are some gaps, the record is largely complete. The most recent gaps were one-month gaps occurring June and August of 2005. The station "Richfield" is 20 km west of CRMO and has been active since 1910. Other long data records are provided by "Arco," 15 km northeast of CRMO (1914-present) and "Jerome," 40 km southwest of CRMO (1915-present). The only significant data gap at the COOP station "Jerome" occurred in April, 1986.

Stations from several weather/climate networks provide near-real-time data within 40 km of the boundaries of CRMO. The main weather/climate networks represented by these stations are ARL FRD, RAWS, SAO, and SNOTEL. In addition to these, stations affiliated with CWOP, ITD, and UPR also currently provide near-real-time weather data in the region.

The bulk of the weather/climate stations in the network run by the ARL FRD are fairly close to CRMO (Figure 4.5). In fact, we identified 19 ARL FRD stations within 40 km of the boundary of CRMO. Most of these stations are north and east of CRMO. All of the stations currently provide near-real-time data for the region.

We identified six active RAWS stations within 40 km of the boundaries of CRMO (Figure 4.5; Table 4.6). The three closest RAWS stations are "Arco", "Crystal", and "Rock Lake". "Arco", located 15 km northeast of CRMO, has been active since 1986. The RAWS station "Crystal" is located just southeast of CRMO and has been active since 1985. "Rock Lake" is located 20 km west of CRMO and has been active since 1990.

We identified five active SAO stations within 40 km of the boundaries of CRMO (Figure 4.5; Table 4.6). With the exception of the SAO station "Hailey Friedman Memorial," which is 40 km northwest of CRMO, most of the SAO stations are south and west of CRMO, with the closest station located at Minidoka Dam, about 15 km southwest of CRMO. In addition, the SAO station at Minidoka Dam also has the longest record of these SAO stations, going back to 1947.

Four SNOTEL stations were identified within 40 km of CRMO boundaries (Figure 4.5; Table 4.6). Three of these are located in the Pioneer Mountains, 30 km northwest of CRMO. The remaining SNOTEL station, "Howell Canyon," which has been discussed previously, is located about 40 km southwest of the southern edge of CRMO.

There are no weather/climate stations located within HAFO (Table 4.6). Seven active COOP stations are located within 40 km of HAFO. The closest active COOP station is "Hagerman 2 SW," located just outside HAFO (Figure 4.5). This station has operated since 1982 and has a reliable data record. The station "Glenns Ferry," which is almost 40 km northwest of HAFO, has the longest record of these active COOP stations, going back to 1905. However, the data record at "Glenns Ferry" has not been very reliable over the years. There are generally no weekend (Saturday-Sunday) observations after 1990, especially during the fall-spring months. The COOP stations "Buhl No 2" and "Jerome," both discussed previously, provide more-reliable long-term records for HAFO.

In addition to these COOP stations, the SAO and COOP stations at King Hill, Idaho also provide long data records, going back to 1933 (Table 4.6). King Hill is about 40 km northwest of HAFO (Figure 4.5). The data records from these two stations are quite reliable. Besides the SAO station at King Hill, there are two other automated stations within 40 km of HAFO. The SAO station "Jerome Co. Arpt." is 30 km east of HAFO and has been active since 1996. The RAWS station "Twin Buttes" is 20 km west of HAFO and has been active since 1990.

No weather/climate stations are located within MIIN (Table 4.6). Nine active COOP stations are located within 40 km of MIIN. The previously-discussed station "Shoshone 1 WNW," which is almost 30 km northwest of MIIN (Figure 4.5), has the longest record of these active COOP stations. The COOP station "Jerome," also discussed previously, is located about 20 km west of MIIN. The COOP station "Hazelton" is located about 15 km southeast of MIIN and has a data record going back to 1917. Although this data record is mostly complete, there are occasional data gaps. The last gaps of note were multi-month gaps in June-July of 1994 and August-September of 1995. The COOP stations "Paul 1 ENE" and "Burley 1 S," both 30 km east of MIIN, also provide reliable data records for the park unit, going back to the 1920s.

We have identified three automated stations providing near-real-time weather data within 40 km of MIIN (Table 4.6; Figure 4.5). Two of these stations are SAO stations. The SAO station "Twin Falls Sun Valley Reg. Arpt." is 30 km southwest of MIIN and has been active since 1948. The SAO station "Jerome Co. Arpt." is about 20 km west of MIIN and has been active since 1996. The RAWS station "Rock Lake," discussed previously, is about 40 km northeast of MIIN.

Table 4.6. Weather/climate stations for UCBN park units in southern Idaho. Stations inside park units and within 40 km of park unit boundaries are included. Missing entries are indicated by "M".

Name	Lat.	Lon.	Elev. (m)	Network	Start	End	In Park?
City of Rocks National Reserve - CIRO							
Albion	42.417	-113.583	1449	COOP	11/1/1899	8/1/1953	NO
Bridge	42.133	-113.350	1434	COOP	8/1/1948	11/30/1952	NO
Grouse Creek 4 NE	41.750	-113.850	1671	COOP	4/13/1982	8/16/1982	NO
Malta	42.302	-113.335	1384	COOP	11/1/1952	Present	NO
Malta 4 ESE	42.292	-113.304	1399	COOP	9/1/1963	11/18/2002	NO
Oakley	42.234	-113.898	1390	COOP	7/1/1893	Present	NO
Rosette	41.819	-113.413	1733	COOP	4/25/1990	Present	NO
Standrod	41.983	-113.267	1708	COOP	1/1/1910	12/31/1942	NO
Strevell	42.017	-113.250	1609	COOP	7/1/1928	2/1/1987	NO
Badger Gulch	42.100	-114.167	2030	NRCS-SC	1/1/1947	Present	NO
Boy Scout Camp	42.217	-113.667	2359	NRCS-SC	1/1/1936	Present	NO

Name	Lat.	Lon.	Elev. (m)	Network	Start	End	In Park?
George Creek	41.900	-113.483	2694	NRCS-SC	1/1/1981	Present	NO
Logger Springs	42.150	-113.733	2475	NRCS-SC	1/1/1979	Present	NO
Vipont	41.900	-113.850	2338	NRCS-SC	1/1/1962	Present	NO
Goose Creek	42.095	-113.896	1725	RAWS	6/1/1990	Present	NO
Malta	42.302	-113.335	1384	SAO	11/1/1952	Present	NO
Strevell	42.017	-113.250	1609	SAO	7/1/1928	2/1/1987	NO
Bostetter R.S.	42.167	-114.183	2286	SNOTEL	10/1/1980	Present	NO
Howell Canyon	42.317	-113.617	2432	SNOTEL	10/1/1980	Present	NO
Craters of the Moon National Park and Preserve – CRMO							
Craters Of The Moon	43.420	-113.540	1800	ARL FRD	M	Present	YES
Arco 17 SW	43.462	-113.556	1804	COOP	7/10/2003	Present	YES
Craters Of The Moon	43.465	-113.558	1797	COOP	11/1/1958	Present	YES
Craters of the Moon	43.461	-113.562	1815	GPMP	9/1/1992	Present	YES
Potter Butte	43.226	-113.574	1503	RAWS	6/1/1990	Present	YES
Aberdeen	42.953	-112.827	1341	Agrimet	1/1/2001	5/31/2002	NO
Malta	42.438	-113.414	1344	Agrimet	6/1/2001	12/31/2001	NO
Picabo	43.312	-114.166	1494	Agrimet	6/1/2001	12/31/2001	NO
Rupert	42.595	-113.838	1266	Agrimet	6/1/2001	12/31/2001	NO
Twin Falls (Kimberly)	42.546	-114.345	1195	Agrimet	6/1/2001	12/31/2001	NO
Aberdeen	43.030	-112.810	1330	ARL FRD	M	Present	NO
Arco	43.620	-113.300	1607	ARL FRD	M	Present	NO
Atomic City	43.430	-112.810	1542	ARL FRD	M	Present	NO
Big Southern Butte	43.290	-113.180	1565	ARL FRD	M	Present	NO
Central Facility	43.530	-112.950	1493	ARL FRD	M	Present	NO
Dead Man Canyon	43.620	-113.060	1541	ARL FRD	M	Present	NO
Experimental Field Station	43.605	-112.907	1487	ARL FRD	M	Present	NO
Grid III	43.590	-112.940	1476	ARL FRD	M	Present	NO
Howe	43.780	-112.980	1457	ARL FRD	M	Present	NO
Howe Peak Base	43.680	-113.000	1481	ARL FRD	M	Present	NO
Lost River Rest Area	43.550	-113.010	1518	ARL FRD	M	Present	NO
Main Gate	43.511	-112.899	1509	ARL FRD	M	Present	NO
Minidoka	42.800	-113.590	1295	ARL FRD	M	Present	NO
Naval Reactor Facility	43.650	-112.910	1462	ARL FRD	M	Present	NO
Power Burst Facility	43.560	-112.910	1476	ARL FRD	M	Present	NO
Rdioactv. Wste. Mgmt. Cplx.	43.500	-113.040	1517	ARL FRD	M	Present	NO
Richfield	43.060	-114.130	1301	ARL FRD	M	Present	NO
Sum	43.396	-113.022	2309	ARL FRD	M	Present	NO
Test Reactor Area	43.580	-112.970	1487	ARL FRD	M	Present	NO
Aberdeen Exp. Stn.	42.954	-112.825	1343	COOP	4/7/1914	Present	NO
Albion	42.417	-113.583	1449	COOP	11/1/1899	8/1/1953	NO
American Falls 3 NW	42.791	-112.921	1343	COOP	12/1/1892	Present	NO
Arco	43.636	-113.299	1623	COOP	3/20/1914	Present	NO

Name	Lat.	Lon.	Elev. (m)	Network	Start	End	In Park?
Bliss 4 NW	42.954	-115.013	998	COOP	12/1/1894	5/17/2004	NO
Bridge	42.133	-113.350	1434	COOP	8/1/1948	11/30/1952	NO
Buhl No 2	42.601	-114.745	1158	COOP	5/18/1906	Present	NO
Burley 2 S	42.519	-113.803	1376	COOP	1/1/1925	Present	NO
Carey	43.283	-113.933	1458	COOP	9/1/1968	11/13/1984	NO
Carey 2 S	43.283	-113.950	1452	COOP	7/1/1956	4/30/1958	NO
Carey 3 NNW	43.350	-113.950	1476	COOP	10/23/1962	9/20/1968	NO
Dry Fork Summit	43.583	-113.683	2227	COOP	9/1/1969	7/31/1976	NO
Eden Hunt Project	42.683	-114.250	1208	COOP	4/1/1943	5/31/1952	NO
Gooding 1 S	42.918	-114.696	1085	COOP	8/27/1952	Present	NO
Gooding 2 S	42.917	-114.717	1088	COOP	4/15/1987	7/1/1998	NO
Gooding Municipal Arpt.	42.917	-114.767	1127	COOP	9/1/1909	4/30/1981	NO
Grouse	43.719	-113.547	1829	COOP	9/1/1932	3/23/2004	NO
Gunnell Guard Stn.	42.100	-113.200	1793	COOP	9/1/1916	9/30/1976	NO
Hagerman 2 SW	42.804	-114.919	876	COOP	5/7/1982	Present	NO
Hailey	43.519	-114.303	1619	COOP	1/12/2005	Present	NO
Hailey 2	43.519	-114.322	1614	COOP	3/1/1966	Present	NO
Hailey Friedman Memorial	43.500	-114.300	1617	COOP	6/1/1953	Present	NO
Hazelton	42.597	-114.138	1237	COOP	5/1/1917	Present	NO
Howe	43.783	-113.003	1469	COOP	2/1/1914	Present	NO
Hunt	42.683	-114.250	0	COOP	9/1/1963	Present	NO
Idaho Falls 46 W	43.532	-112.942	1505	COOP	1/1/1952	Present	NO
Jerome	42.733	-114.519	1140	COOP	9/1/1915	Present	NO
Little Wood Dam	43.433	-114.017	1592	COOP	11/1/1960	10/31/1962	NO
Magic Dam Outflow	43.251	-114.371	1422	COOP	8/1/1976	Present	NO
Magic Lake Resort	43.283	-114.383	1464	COOP	6/1/1966	10/10/1975	NO
Malta	42.302	-113.335	1384	COOP	11/1/1952	Present	NO
Malta 4 ESE	42.292	-113.304	1399	COOP	9/1/1963	11/18/2002	NO
Massacre Rocks St. Park	42.668	-112.998	1279	COOP	4/1/1973	Present	NO
Milner Dam	42.533	-114.117	1281	COOP	1/1/1904	12/31/1946	NO
Minidoka 10 WNW	42.783	-113.667	1308	COOP	11/11/1895	5/31/1988	NO
Minidoka Dam	42.677	-113.500	1269	COOP	5/2/1947	Present	NO
Mosby Butte	43.083	-113.083	0	COOP	9/1/1963	Present	NO
Mosby Butte Look Out	43.050	-113.133	1678	COOP	7/1/1956	Present	NO
Neeley	42.767	-112.883	1293	COOP	8/1/1948	5/31/1978	NO
Notch Butte Look Out	42.883	-114.400	1366	COOP	7/1/1953	Present	NO
Oakley	42.234	-113.898	1390	COOP	7/1/1893	Present	NO
Paul 1 ENE	42.628	-113.762	1265	COOP	1/1/1925	Present	NO
Picabo	43.311	-114.074	1472	COOP	4/1/1958	Present	NO
Richfield	43.053	-114.158	1305	COOP	2/1/1910	Present	NO
Rockland	42.514	-112.875	1433	COOP	11/1/2001	Present	NO
Rupert 13 NNE	42.800	-113.567	1327	COOP	7/1/1962	10/1/1966	NO
Rupert 3 WSW	42.604	-113.758	1280	COOP	11/1/1906	6/26/2002	NO

Name	Lat.	Lon.	Elev. (m)	Network	Start	End	In Park?
Shoshone 1 WNW	42.938	-114.417	1204	COOP	3/1/1908	Present	NO
Slick Rock	43.667	-113.867	2638	COOP	10/1/1966	9/30/1969	NO
Standrod	41.983	-113.267	1708	COOP	1/1/1910	12/31/1942	NO
Strevell	42.017	-113.250	1609	COOP	7/1/1928	2/1/1987	NO
Twin Falls 2 NNE	42.583	-114.467	1125	COOP	9/1/1905	5/31/1974	NO
Twin Falls 3 SE	42.533	-114.417	1150	COOP	1/1/1925	6/30/1977	NO
Twin Falls 6 E	42.546	-114.346	1207	COOP	4/1/1962	Present	NO
Twin Falls KMVT	42.581	-114.457	1119	COOP	7/16/1960	Present	NO
CW3797 Filer	42.500	-114.700	1141	CWOP	M	Present	NO
CW4995 Bliss	42.946	-115.014	1014	CWOP	M	Present	NO
Coldwater	42.634	-113.091	1286	ITD	M	Present	NO
Glenns Ferry	42.944	-115.117	908	ITD	M	Present	NO
Hansen Bridge	42.570	-114.390	1219	ITD	M	Present	NO
Perrine Bridge	42.630	-114.450	1128	ITD	M	Present	NO
Raft River	42.580	-113.440	1310	ITD	M	Present	NO
Ridgeway	42.570	-113.970	1341	ITD	M	Present	NO
Sterling	43.045	-112.740	1335	ITD	M	Present	NO
Yale	42.520	-113.420	1326	ITD	M	Present	NO
Boy Scout Camp	42.217	-113.667	2359	NRCS-SC	1/1/1936	Present	NO
Dry Fork	43.583	-113.683	2201	NRCS-SC	1/1/1967	Present	NO
Fishpole Lake	43.650	-113.850	2835	NRCS-SC	1/1/1968	Present	NO
George Creek	41.900	-113.483	2694	NRCS-SC	1/1/1981	Present	NO
Iron Mine Creek	43.550	-113.717	1920	NRCS-SC	1/1/1958	Present	NO
Logger Springs	42.150	-113.733	2475	NRCS-SC	1/1/1979	Present	NO
Muldoon	43.567	-113.917	1926	NRCS-SC	1/1/1953	Present	NO
Telfer Ranch	43.533	-113.767	1780	NRCS-SC	1/1/1953	Present	NO
Arco	43.623	-113.387	1640	RAWS	11/1/1986	Present	NO
Copper Basin	43.800	-113.833	2384	RAWS	1/1/1985	Present	NO
Crystal	42.990	-113.160	1544	RAWS	1/1/1985	Present	NO
Goose Creek	42.095	-113.896	1725	RAWS	6/1/1990	Present	NO
Lake Hills	43.451	-113.908	1823	RAWS	6/1/1990	5/31/1997	NO
Raft River	42.548	-113.259	1341	RAWS	11/1/1986	Present	NO
Rock Lake	42.972	-114.063	1298	RAWS	7/1/1990	Present	NO
Starlight	42.693	-112.689	1585	RAWS	7/1/1990	5/31/1997	NO
Gooding Municipal Arpt.	42.917	-114.767	1127	SAO	9/1/1909	4/30/1981	NO
Hailey Friedman Memorial	43.500	-114.300	1617	SAO	6/1/1953	Present	NO
Jerome Co. Arpt.	42.727	-114.456	1234	SAO	12/26/1996	Present	NO
Malta	42.302	-113.335	1384	SAO	11/1/1952	Present	NO
Minidoka Dam	42.677	-113.500	1269	SAO	5/2/1947	Present	NO
Strevell	42.017	-113.250	1609	SAO	7/1/1928	2/1/1987	NO
Twin Falls Sun Valley Reg. Arpt.	42.482	-114.487	1265	SAO	5/1/1948	Present	NO
Bear Canyon	43.750	-113.933	2408	SNOTEL	10/1/1980	Present	NO

Name	Lat.	Lon.	Elev. (m)	Network	Start	End	In Park?
Garfield R.S.	43.617	-113.933	1999	SNOTEL	10/1/1980	Present	NO
Howell Canyon	42.317	-113.617	2432	SNOTEL	10/1/1980	Present	NO
Swede Peak	43.617	-113.967	2329	SNOTEL	10/1/1981	Present	NO
Bannock	42.837	-112.772	1345	UPR	M	Present	NO
Bliss	42.925	-115.020	974	UPR	M	Present	NO
Dietrich	42.908	-114.262	1244	UPR	M	Present	NO
Gooding	42.951	-114.634	1107	UPR	M	Present	NO
Hawley	42.742	-113.434	1319	UPR	M	Present	NO
Kimama	42.841	-113.800	1295	UPR	M	Present	NO
Quigley	42.731	-113.107	1348	UPR	M	Present	NO
Kimberly	42.533	-114.350	254	WBAN	M	Present	NO
Hagerman Fossil Beds National Monument – HAFO							
Glenns Ferry	42.867	-115.357	922	Agrimet	6/1/2001	12/31/2001	NO
Bliss 4 NW	42.954	-115.013	998	COOP	12/1/1894	5/17/2004	NO
Buhl No 2	42.601	-114.745	1158	COOP	5/18/1906	Present	NO
Castleford 2 N	42.550	-114.866	1166	COOP	6/1/1963	Present	NO
Glenns Ferry	42.940	-115.323	752	COOP	1/1/1905	Present	NO
Gooding 1 S	42.918	-114.696	1085	COOP	8/27/1952	Present	NO
Gooding 2 S	42.917	-114.717	1088	COOP	4/15/1987	7/1/1998	NO
Gooding Municipal Arpt.	42.917	-114.767	1127	COOP	9/1/1909	4/30/1981	NO
Hagerman 2 SW	42.804	-114.919	876	COOP	5/7/1982	Present	NO
Jerome	42.733	-114.519	1140	COOP	9/1/1915	Present	NO
King Hill	43.000	-115.200	0	COOP	3/1/1933	Present	NO
King Hill CAA Arpt.	42.983	-115.200	836	COOP	1/1/1933	12/31/1941	NO
CW3797 Filer	42.500	-114.700	1141	CWOP	M	Present	NO
CW4995 Bliss	42.946	-115.014	1014	CWOP	M	Present	NO
Glenns Ferry	42.944	-115.117	908	ITD	M	Present	NO
Twin Buttes	42.691	-115.195	1021	RAWS	5/1/1990	Present	NO
Gooding Municipal Arpt.	42.917	-114.767	1127	SAO	9/1/1909	4/30/1981	NO
Jerome Co. Arpt.	42.727	-114.456	1234	SAO	12/26/1996	Present	NO
King Hill	43.000	-115.200	0	SAO	3/1/1933	Present	NO
Bliss	42.925	-115.020	974	UPR	M	Present	NO
Gooding	42.951	-114.634	1107	UPR	M	Present	NO
Minidoka Internment National Monument – MIIN							
Rupert	42.595	-113.838	1266	Agrimet	6/1/2001	12/31/2001	NO
Twin Falls (Kimberly)	42.546	-114.345	1195	Agrimet	6/1/2001	12/31/2001	NO
Burley 2 S	42.519	-113.803	1376	COOP	1/1/1925	Present	NO
Eden Hunt Project	42.683	-114.250	1208	COOP	4/1/1943	5/31/1952	NO
Hazelton	42.597	-114.138	1237	COOP	5/1/1917	Present	NO
Hunt	42.683	-114.250	0	COOP	9/1/1963	Present	NO
Jerome	42.733	-114.519	1140	COOP	9/1/1915	Present	NO
Milner Dam	42.533	-114.117	1281	COOP	1/1/1904	12/31/1946	NO
Notch Butte Look Out	42.883	-114.400	1366	COOP	7/1/1953	Present	NO

Name	Lat.	Lon.	Elev. (m)	Network	Start	End	In Park?
Paul 1 ENE	42.628	-113.762	1265	COOP	1/1/1925	Present	NO
Shoshone 1 WNW	42.938	-114.417	1204	COOP	3/1/1908	Present	NO
Twin Falls 2 NNE	42.583	-114.467	1125	COOP	9/1/1905	5/31/1974	NO
Twin Falls 3 SE	42.533	-114.417	1150	COOP	1/1/1925	6/30/1977	NO
Twin Falls 6 E	42.546	-114.346	1207	COOP	4/1/1962	Present	NO
Twin Falls KMVT	42.581	-114.457	1119	COOP	7/16/1960	Present	NO
Hansen Bridge	42.570	-114.390	1219	ITD	M	Present	NO
Perrine Bridge	42.630	-114.450	1128	ITD	M	Present	NO
Ridgeway	42.570	-113.970	1341	ITD	M	Present	NO
Rock Lake	42.972	-114.063	1298	RAWS	7/1/1990	Present	NO
Jerome Co. Arpt.	42.727	-114.456	1234	SAO	12/26/1996	Present	NO
Twin Falls Sun Valley Reg. Arpt.	42.482	-114.487	1265	SAO	5/1/1948	Present	NO
Dietrich	42.908	-114.262	1244	UPR	M	Present	NO
Kimama	42.841	-113.800	1295	UPR	M	Present	NO
Kimberly	42.533	-114.350	254	WBAN	M	Present	NO

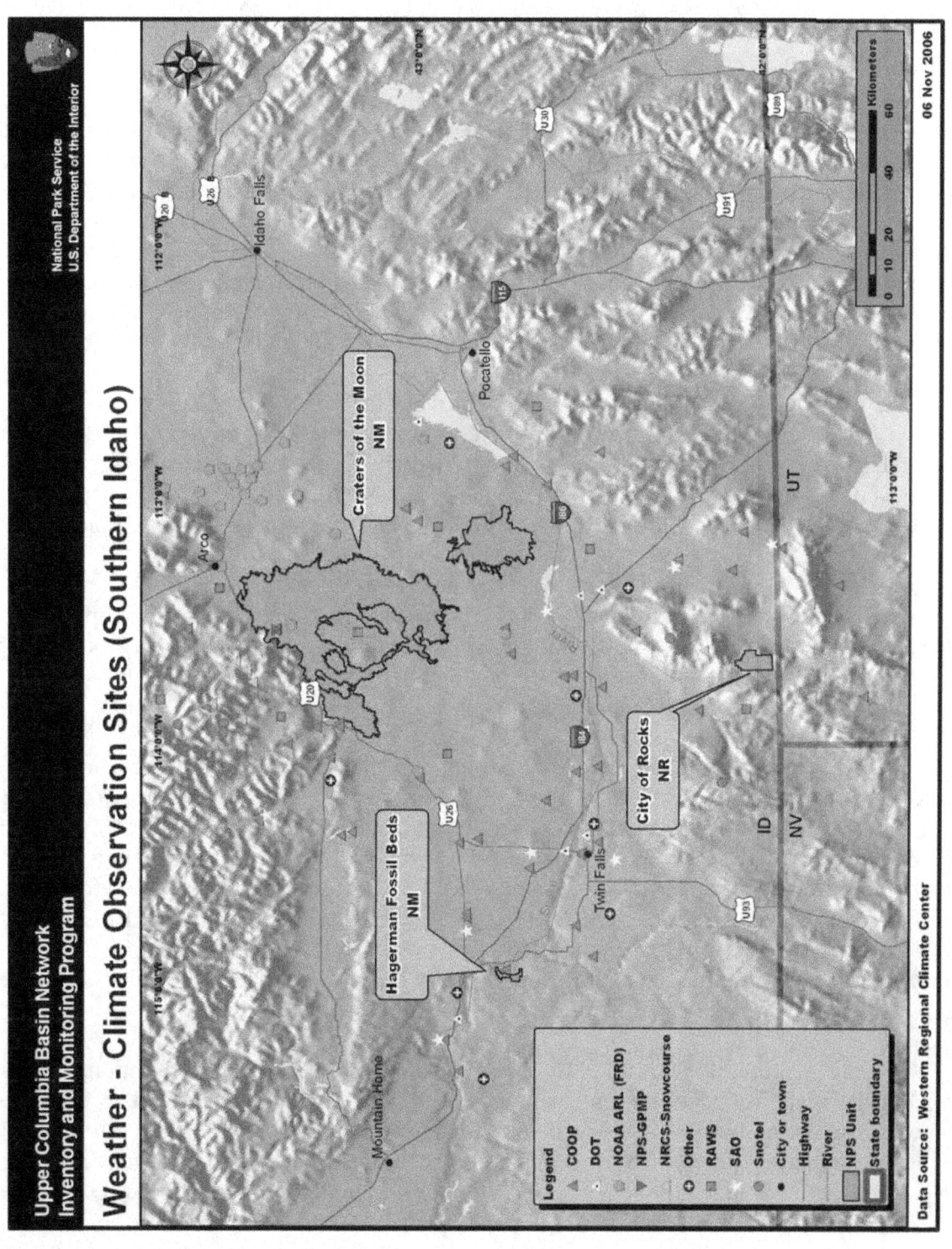

Figure 4.5. Station locations for UCBN park units in southern Idaho.

55

5.0. Conclusions and Recommendations

We have based our findings on an examination of the available records and the topography and climate within UCBN units, discussions with NPS staff and other collaborators, and prior knowledge of the area. Here, we offer an evaluation and general comments pertaining to the status, prospects, and needs for climate-monitoring capabilities in UCBN.

5.1. Upper Columbia Basin Inventory and Monitoring Network

A few of the park units in the UCBN must rely solely on weather and climate stations that are outside of the park units. Park units that fall in this category include, BIHO, CIRO, HAFO, and MIIN. Fortunately, for some of these park units, there appears to be satisfactory coverage of both manual and automated stations. For instance, HAFO has a few stations within 40 km that have reliable long-term climate records. This park unit is also surrounded by three near-real-time stations that are within 40 km. A COOP station with a reliable data record (Hagerman 2 SW) is just outside of HAFO. Another park unit with satisfactory weather/climate station coverage is MIIN. Long-term data records are available at multiple COOP stations within 20 km of MIIN and near-real-time data are available from three stations within 30 km of MIIN.

Other park units that currently have no weather or climate stations could benefit from the installation of additional stations. Big Hole National Battlefield (BIHO) has access to reliable long-term data records through the COOP station "Wisdom." However, all except one of the automated stations we identified for BIHO were not located in the Big Hole Valley. The only automated station we identified in the Big Hole Valley is a RAWS station 35 km northeast of BIHO (Calvert Creek). The NPS might consider installing an automated station at BIHO, such as a RAWS station. This would provide much-needed near-real-time data in the Big Hole Valley that could be used in various environmental studies. Another possible site for an automated station is at Gibbons Pass, 20 km west of BIHO. The NPS might pursue teaming up with NRCS to upgrade the NRCS-SC station that is currently at Gibbons Pass to a SNOTEL site, which would benefit hydrologic studies in the region around BIHO.

Similarly, since CIRO is located in the Albion Mountains, the NPS might consider teaming up with NRCS to upgrade the NRCS-SC station "Boy Scout Camp," which is only 10 km north of CIRO, to a SNOTEL station. Due to the very limited station coverage around CIRO, there are no manual or automated stations within 30 km of CIRO. Almost all of the current stations are located in the lower-elevation basins surrounding the Albion Mountains and are therefore less representative of the local climate at CIRO. The one exception to this is the SNOTEL station "Howell Canyon," which is in the Albion Mountains; however, it is 30 km north of CIRO. An additional automated station in the region would greatly improve weather monitoring efforts for CIRO.

The COOP stations presently within JODA units have data records that are of questionable quality. In particular, the COOP station "Dayville 8 NW" regularly lacks weekend observations. Taking efforts to ensure weekend observations are made at this station will benefit NPS. Installing an automated station such as a RAWS station at one of the JODA units may also be feasible, since there are generally no automated stations within 20 km of any of the JODA units.

The coverage of weather/climate stations in and near LARO appears to be satisfactory. Long-term records are available at several stations near LARO, including COOP stations at the south end of LARO (Coulee 1 SW) and at the north end of LARO (Northport). Near-real-time data are available at two different RAWS stations along Lake Roosevelt, allowing studies of local climate gradients along the Columbia River Valley. Several other RAWS and SAO sites within 40 km of LARO also provide near-real-time weather data. Weather/climate station coverage is satisfactory at WHMI. This park unit has a manual COOP station within the park that now has a reliable data record lasting several decades. In addition, there are numerous stations south and east of WHMI, including the COOP and SAO stations in Walla Walla, 10 km east of WHMI. The coverage of weather/climate stations for the various units of NEPE is satisfactory, in that there are both long-term climate records and near-real-time weather data available within 40 km of each of the NEPE units considered in this report.

Almost all of the manual and automated stations we identified in CRMO are located at or near the main visitor center, in the northern part of the park unit. The only other station within CRMO is the RAWS station "Potter Butte," 10 km southeast of the visitor center. Stations are lacking throughout the rest of CRMO, particularly the southern half of the park unit. The primary automated networks present in the region are ARL FRD and RAWS. NPS could therefore benefit by teaming up with either the ARL FRD network or the RAWS network to install an automated station in the southern half of CRMO. The cost of setting up an ARL FRD station appears to be more expensive than installing a RAWS station (see Appendix F). However, the ARL FRD network is advantageous in that the agency (ARL FRD) responsible for operating and maintaining this network is located in Idaho Falls, which is within 100 km of CRMO.

5.2. Spatial Variations in Mean Climate

Topography is a major controlling factor on the park units within UCBN, leading to systematic spatial variations in mean surface climate. With local variations over short horizontal and vertical distances, topography introduces considerable fine-scale structure to mean climate (temperature and precipitation). Issues encountered in mapping mean climate are discussed in Appendix E and in Redmond et al. (2005).

If only a few stations will be emplaced, the primary goal should be overall characterization of the main climate elements (temperature and precipitation and their joint relative, snow). This level of characterization generally requires that (a) stations should not be located in deep valley bottoms (cold air drainage pockets) or near excessively steep slopes and (b) stations should be distributed spatially in the major biomes of each park. If such stations already are present in the vicinity, then additional stations would be best used for two important and somewhat competing purposes: (a) add redundancy as backup for loss of data from current stations (or loss of the physical stations) or (b) provide added information on spatial heterogeneity in climate arising from topographic diversity.

5.3. Climate Change Detection

The desire for credible, accurate, complete, and long-term climate records—from any location—cannot be overemphasized. Thus, this consideration always should have a high priority. However, because of spatial diversity in climate, monitoring that fills knowledge gaps and provides information on long-term temporal variability in short-distance relationships also will be valuable. We cannot be sure that climate variability and climate change will affect all parts of a given park unit equally. In fact, it is appropriate to speculate that this is not the case, and spatial variations in temporal variability extend to small spatial scales (a few kilometers or less in some cases), a consequence of topographic diversity within UCBN.

5.4. Aesthetics

This issue arises frequently enough to deserve comment. Standards for quality climate measurements require open exposures away from heat sources, buildings, pavement, close vegetation and tall trees, and human intrusion (thus away from property lines). By their nature, sites that meet these standards are usually quite visible. In many settings (such as heavily forested areas) these sites also are quite rare, making them precisely the same places that managers wish to protect from aesthetic intrusion. The most suitable and scientifically defensible sites frequently are rejected as candidate locations for weather/climate stations. Most weather/climate stations, therefore, tend to be "hidden" but many of these hidden locations have inferior exposures. Some measure of compromise is nearly always called for in siting weather and climate stations.

The public has vast interest and curiosity in weather and climate, and within the NPS I&M networks, such measurements consistently rate near or at the top of desired public information. There seem to be many possible opportunities for exploiting and embracing this widespread interest within the interpretive mission of the NPS. One way to do this would be to highlight rather than hide these stations and educate the public about the need for adequate siting. A number of weather displays we have encountered during visits have proven inadvertently to serve as counterexamples for how measurements should not be made.

5.5. Information Access

Access to information promotes its use, which in turn promotes attention to station care and maintenance, better data, and more use. An end-to-end view that extends from sensing to decision support is far preferable to isolated and disconnected activities and aids the support infrastructure that is ultimately so necessary for successful, long-term climate monitoring.

Decisions about improvements in monitoring capacity are facilitated greatly by the ability to examine available climate information. Various methods are being created at WRCC to improve access to that information. Web pages providing historic and ongoing climate data, and information from UCBN park units can be accessed at http://www.wrcc.dri.edu/nps. In the event that this URL changes, there still will be links from the main WRCC Web page entitled "Projects" under NPS.

The WRCC has been steadily developing software to summarize data from hourly sites. This has been occurring under the aegis of the RAWS program and a growing array of product generators ranging from daily and monthly data lists to wind roses and hourly frequency distributions. All park data are available to park personnel via an access code (needed only for data listings) that can be acquired by request. The WRCC RAWS Web page is located at http://www.wrcc.dri.edu/wraws or http://www.raws.dri.edu.

Web pages have been developed to provide access not only to historic and ongoing climate data and information from UCBN park units but also to climate-monitoring efforts for UCBN. These pages can be found through http://www.wrcc.dri.edu/nps.

Additional access to more standard climate information is accessible though the previously mentioned Web pages, as well as through http://www.wrcc.dri.edu/summary. These summaries are generally for COOP stations.

5.6. Summarized Conclusions and Recommendations

- Weather/climate station coverage is generally adequate for HAFO, LARO, MIIN, NEPE, and WHMI.
- Very little near-real-time weather data is available around BIHO. NPS may consider working with NRCS to upgrade NRCS-SC site at Gibbons Pass to a SNOTEL site. Alternatively, consider installing an automated station such as a RAWS station at BIHO.
- The current manual and automated stations around CIRO, generally located in lower-elevation basins, are generally not representative of CIRO, located in Albion Mountains. NPS may consider working with NRCS to upgrade NRCS-SC site "Boy Scout Ranch" to a SNOTEL site.
- The COOP stations presently within JODA units have data records that are of questionable quality. In particular, the COOP station "Dayville 8 NW" regularly lacks weekend observations. Taking efforts to ensure weekend observations are made at this station will benefit NPS. NPS may also consider installing an automated station such as a RAWS station at one of the JODA units, since automated stations are generally not found within 20 km of any of the JODA units.
- Most weather/climate stations within CRMO are located at main visitor center. No stations were identified in the southern portion of the park unit. NPS may consider installing an ARL FRD station or a RAWS station in southern CRMO. A RAWS station is less costly, but maintenance personnel are more accessible for an ARL FRD station.

6.0 Literature Cited

American Association of State Climatologists. 1985. Heights and exposure standards for sensors on automated weather stations. The State Climatologist **9**.

Bonan, G. B. 2002. Ecological Climatology: Concepts and Applications. Cambridge University Press.

Bureau of Land Management. 1997. Remote Automatic Weather Station (RAWS) and Remote Environmental Monitoring Systems (REMS) standards. RAWS/REMS Support Facility, Boise, Idaho.

Cayan, D. R., M. D. Dettinger, H. F Diaz, and N. E. Graham. 1998. Decadal variability of precipitation over western North America. Journal of Climate **11**:3148-3166.

Chapin, F. S. III, M. S. Torn, and M. Tateno. 1996. Principles of ecosystem sustainability. The American Naturalist **148**:1016-1037.

D'Antonio, C. M. 2000. Fire, plant invasions, and global changes. Pages 65-93 *in* Mooney, H. A. and R. J. Hobbs, editors. Invasive species in a changing world. Island Press, Washington, D.C.

Daly, C., R. P. Neilson, and D. L. Phillips. 1994. A statistical-topographic model for mapping climatological precipitation over mountainous terrain. Journal of Applied Meteorology **33**:140-158.

Daly, C., W. P. Gibson, G. H. Taylor, G. L. Johnson, and P. Pasteris. 2002. A knowledge-based approach to the statistical mapping of climate. Climate Research **22**:99-113.

Doggett, M., C. Daly, J. Smith, W. Gibson, G. Taylor, G. Johnson, and P. Pasteris. 2004. High-resolution 1971-2000 mean monthly temperature maps for the western United States. Fourteenth AMS Conf. on Applied Climatology, 84th AMS Annual Meeting. Seattle, WA, American Meteorological Society, Boston, MA, January 2004, Paper 4.3, CD-ROM.

Environmental Protection Agency. 1987. On-site meteorological program guidance for regulatory modeling applications. EPA-450/4-87-013. Environmental Protection Agency, Office of Air Quality Planning and Standards, Research Triangle Park, NC.

Ferguson, S. A. 1999. Climatology of the Interior Columbia River Basin. USDA Forest Service, Pacific Northwest Research Station, Portland, Oregon. General Technical Report PNW-GTR-445.

Finklin, A. I., and W. C. Fischer. 1990. Weather station handbook –an interagency guide for wildland managers. NFES No. 2140. National Wildfire Coordinating Group, Boise, Idaho.

Garrett, L., T. Rodhouse, L. Svancara, and C. C. Caudill. 2005. Phase II Vital Signs Monitoring Plan: Upper Columbia Basin Network. National Park Service, Upper Columbia Basin Network, National Park Service Inventory and Monitoring Program, Moscow, Idaho.

Gibson, W. P., C. Daly, T. Kittel, D. Nychka, C. Johns, N. Rosenbloom, A. McNab, and G. Taylor. 2002. Development of a 103-year high-resolution climate data set for the conterminous United States. Thirteenth AMS Conf. on Applied Climatology. Portland, OR, American Meteorological Society, Boston, MA, May 2002:181-183.

Hessl, A. E., D. McKenzie, and R. Schellhaas. 2004. Drought and Pacific Decadal Oscillation linked to fire occurrence in the inland Pacific Northwest. Ecological Applications **14**:425-442.

Heyerdahl, E. K., L. B. Brubaker, and J. K. Agee. 2002. Annual and decadal climate forcing of historical fire regimes in the interior Pacific Northwest, USA. The Holocene **12**:597-604.

I&M. 2006. I&M Inventories home page. http://science.nature.nps.gov/im/inventory/index.cfm.

Jacobson, M. C., R. J. Charlson, H. Rodhe, and G. H. Orians. 2000. Earth System Science: From Biogeochemical Cycles to Global Change. Academic Press, San Diego.

Karl, T. R., V. E. Derr, D. R. Easterling, C. K. Folland, D. J. Hoffman, S. Levitus, N. Nicholls, D. E. Parker, and G. W. Withee. 1996. Critical issues for long-term climate monitoring. Pages 55-92 *in* T. R. Karl, editor. Long Term Climate Monitoring by the Global Climate Observing System, Kluwer Publishing.

Logan, J. A., and J. A. Powell. 2001. Ghost forests, global warming, and the mountain pine beetle. American Entomologist **47**:160-172.

Mantua, N. J., S. R. Hare, Y. Zhang, J. M. Wallace, and R. C. Francis. 1997. A Pacific interdecadal climate oscillation with impacts on salmon production. Bulletin of the American Meteorological Society **78**:1069-1079.

Mantua, N. J. 2000. The Pacific Decadal Oscillation and climate forecasting for North America. Online. (http://www.atmos.washington.edu/~mantua/REPORTS/PDO/PDO_cs.htm) Accessed 27 April 2004.

McKenzie, D., Z. Gedalof, D. L. Peterson, and P. Mote. 2004. Climate change, wildfire, and conservation. Conservation Biology **18**:890-902.

Melack, J. M., J. Dozier, C. R. Goldman, D. Greenland, A. M. Milner, and R. J. Naiman. 1997. Effects of climate change on inland waters of the coastal mountains and western great basin of North America. Hydrological Processes **11**:971-992.

Mock, C. J. 1996. Climatic controls and spatial variations of precipitation in the western United States. Journal of Climate **9**:1111-1125.

Mote, P. W., A. F. Hamlet, M. P. Clark, and D. P. Lettenmaier. 2005. Declining mountain snowpack in western North America. Bulletin of the American Meteorological Society **86**:39-49.

National Assessment Synthesis Team. 2001. Climate Change Impacts on the United States: The Potential Consequences of Climate Variability and Change, Report for the U.S. Global Change Research Program. Cambridge University Press, Cambridge, UK.

National Research Council. 2001. A Climate Services Vision: First Steps Toward the Future. National Academies Press, Washington, D.C.

National Wildfire Coordinating Group. 2004. National fire danger rating system weather station standards. Report PMS 426.3. National Wildfire Coordinating Group, Boise, Idaho.

Neilson, R. P. 1987. Biotic regionalization and climatic controls in western North America. Vegetatio **70**:135-147.

Oakley, K. L., L. P. Thomas, and S. G. Fancy. 2003. Guidelines for long-term monitoring protocols. Wildlife Society Bulletin **31**:1000-1003.

Quigley, T. M. and S. J. Arbelbide, editors. 1997. An assessment of ecosystem components in the Interior Columbia Basin and portions of the Klamath and Great Basins, Volumes I-III. USDA Forest Service, Pacific Northwest Research Station, Portland, Oregon. General Technical Report PNW-GTR-405.

Redmond, K. T., and R. W. Koch. 1991. Surface climate and streamflow variability in the western United States and their relationship to large-scale circulation indices. Water Resources Research **27**:2381-2399.

Redmond, K. T., D. B. Simeral, and G. D. McCurdy. 2005. Climate monitoring for southwest Alaska national parks: network design and site selection. Report 05-01. Western Regional Climate Center, Reno, Nevada.

Schlesinger, W. H. 1997. Biogeochemistry: An Analysis of Global Change. Academic Press, San Diego.

Smith, S. D., T. E. Huxman, S. F. Zitzer, T. N. Charlet, D. C. Housman, J. S. Coleman, L. K. Fenstermaker, J. R. Seemann, and R. S. Nowak. 2000. Elevated CO_2 increases productivity and invasive species success in an arid ecosystem. Nature **408**:79-82.

Tanner, B. D. 1990. Automated weather stations. Remote Sensing Reviews **5**:73-98.

Wagner, F. H., R. Angell, M. Hahn, T. Lawlor, R. Tausch, and D. Toweill. 2003. Natural ecosystems III. The Great Basin. Pages 207-240 *in* Wagner, F. H., editor. Rocky

Mountain/Great Basin regional climate-change assessment. Report for the U.S. global change research program. Utah State University, Logan, Utah.

Wallace, J. M., and D. S. Gutzler. 1981. Teleconnections in the geopotential height field during the Northern Hemisphere winter. Monthly Weather Review **109**:784-812.

Whitlock, C., S. L. Shafer, and J. Marlon. 2003. The role of climate and vegetation change in shaping past and future fire regimes in the northwestern US and the implications for ecosystem management. Forest Ecology and Management **178**:5-21.

World Meteorological Organization. 1983. Guide to Meteorological Instruments and Methods of Observation, No. 8, 5th edition, World Meteorological Organization, Geneva Switzerland.

World Meteorological Organization. 2005. Organization and planning of intercomparisons of rainfall intensity gauges. World Meteorological Organization, Geneva Switzerland.

Appendix A. Climate-monitoring principles

Since the late 1990s, frequent references have been made to a set of climate-monitoring principles enunciated in 1996 by Tom Karl, director of the NOAA NCDC in Asheville, North Carolina. These monitoring principles also have been referred to informally as the "Ten Commandments of Climate Monitoring." Both versions are given here. In addition, these principles have been adopted by the Global Climate Observing System (GCOS 2004).

(Compiled by Kelly Redmond, Western Regional Climate Center, Desert Research Institute, August 2000.)

A.1. Full Version (Karl et al. 1996)

A.1.1. Effects on climate records of instrument changes, observing practices, observation locations, sampling rates, etc., must be known before such changes are implemented. This can be ascertained through a period where overlapping measurements from old and new observing systems are collected or sometimes by comparing the old and new observing systems with a reference standard. Site stability for in situ measurements, both in terms of physical location and changes in the nearby environment, also should be a key criterion in site selection. Thus, many synoptic network stations, which are primarily used in weather forecasting but also provide valuable climate data, and dedicated climate stations intended to be operational for extended periods must be subject to this policy.

A.1.2. Processing algorithms and changes in these algorithms must be well documented. Documentation should be carried with the data throughout the data-archiving process.

A.1.3. Knowledge of instrument, station, and/or platform history is essential for interpreting and using the data. Changes in instrument sampling time, local environmental conditions for in situ measurements, and other factors pertinent to interpreting the observations and measurements should be recorded as a mandatory part in the observing routine and be archived with the original data.

A.1.4. In situ and other observations with a long, uninterrupted record should be maintained. Every effort should be applied to protect the data sets that have provided long-term, homogeneous observations. "Long-term" for space-based measurements is measured in decades, but for more conventional measurements, "long-term" may be a century or more. Each element in the observational system should develop a list of prioritized sites or observations based on their contribution to long-term climate monitoring.

A.1.5. Calibration, validation, and maintenance facilities are critical requirements for long-term climatic data sets. Homogeneity in the climate record must be assessed routinely, and corrective action must become part of the archived record.

A.1.6. Where feasible, some level of "low-technology" backup to "high-technology" observing systems should be developed to safeguard against unexpected operational failures.

A.1.7. Regions having insufficient data, variables and regions sensitive to change, and key measurements lacking adequate spatial and temporal resolution should be given the highest priority in designing and implementing new climate-observing systems.

A.1.8. Network designers and instrument engineers must receive long-term climate requirements at the outset of the network design process. This is particularly important because most observing systems have been designed for purposes other than long-term climate monitoring. Instruments must possess adequate accuracy with biases small enough to document climate variations and changes.

A.1.9. Much of the development of new observational capabilities and the evidence supporting the value of these observations stem from research-oriented needs or programs. A lack of stable, long-term commitment to these observations and lack of a clear transition plan from research to operations are two frequent limitations in the development of adequate, long-term monitoring capabilities. Difficulties in securing a long-term commitment must be overcome in order to improve the climate-observing system in a timely manner with minimal interruptions.

A.1.10. Data management systems that facilitate access, use, and interpretation are essential. Freedom of access, low cost, mechanisms that facilitate use (directories, catalogs, browse capabilities, availability of metadata on station histories, algorithm accessibility and documentation, etc.) and quality control should guide data management. International cooperation is critical for successful management of data used to monitor long-term climate change and variability.

A.2. Abbreviated version, "Ten Commandments of Climate Monitoring"

A.2.1. Assess the impact of new climate-observing systems or changes to existing systems before they are implemented.

"Thou shalt properly manage network change." (assess effects of proposed changes)

A.2.2. Require a suitable period where measurement from new and old climate-observing systems will overlap.

"Thou shalt conduct parallel testing." (compare old and replacement systems)

A.2.3. Treat calibration, validation, algorithm-change, and data-homogeneity assessments with the same care as the data.

"Thou shalt collect metadata." (fully document system and operating procedures)

A.2.4. Verify capability for routinely assessing the quality and homogeneity of the data including high-resolution data for extreme events.

"Thou shalt assure data quality and continuity." (assess as part of routine operating procedures)

A.2.5. Integrate assessments like those conducted by the International Panel on Climate Change into global climate-observing priorities.

"Thou shalt anticipate the use of data." (integrated environmental assessment; component in operational plan for system)

A.2.6. Maintain long-term weather and climate stations.

"Thou shalt worship historic significance." (maintain homogeneous data sets from long–term, climate-observing systems)

A.2.7. Place high priority on increasing observations in regions lacking sufficient data and in regions sensitive to change and variability.

"Thou shalt acquire complementary data." (new sites to fill observational gaps)

A.2.8. Provide network operators, designers, and instrument engineers with long-term requirements at the outset of the design and implementation phases for new systems.

"Thou shalt specify requirements for climate observation systems." (application and usage of observational data)

A.2.9. Carefully consider the transition from research-observing system to long-term operation.

"Thou shalt have continuity of purpose." (stable long-term commitments)

A.2.10. Focus on data-management systems that facilitate access, use, and interpretation of weather data and metadata.

"Thou shalt provide access to data and metadata." (readily available weather and climate information)

A.3. Literature Cited

Karl, T. R., V. E. Derr, D. R. Easterling, C. K. Folland, D. J. Hoffman, S. Levitus, N. Nicholls, D. E. Parker, and G. W. Withee. 1996. Critical Issues for Long-Term Climate Monitoring. Pages 55-92 *in* T. R. Karl, editor. Long Term Climate Monitoring by the Global Climate Observing System, Kluwer Publishing.

Global Climate Observing System. 2004. Implementation Plan for the Global Observing System for Climate in Support of the UNFCCC. GCOS-92, WMO/TD No. 1219, World Meteorological Organization, Geneva, Switzerland.

Appendix B. Glossary

Climate—Complete and entire ensemble of statistical descriptors of temporal and spatial properties comprising the behavior of the atmosphere. These descriptors include means, variances, frequency distributions, autocorrelations, spatial correlations and other patterns of association, temporal lags, and element-to-element relationships. The descriptors have a physical basis in flows and reservoirs of energy and mass. Climate and weather phenomena shade gradually into each other and are ultimately inseparable.

Climate Element—(same as Weather Element) Attribute or property of the state of the atmosphere that is measured, estimated, or derived. Examples of climate elements include temperature, wind speed, wind direction, precipitation amount, precipitation type, relative humidity, dewpoint, solar radiation, snow depth, soil temperature at a given depth, etc. A derived element is a function of other elements (like degree days or number of days with rain) and is not measured directly with a sensor. The terms "parameter" or "variable" are not used to describe elements.

Climate Network—Group of climate stations having a common purpose; the group is often owned and maintained by a single organization.

Climate Station—Station where data are collected to track atmospheric conditions over the long-term. Often, this station operates to additional standards to verify long-term consistency. For these stations, the detailed circumstances surrounding a set of measurements (siting and exposure, instrument changes, etc.) are important.

Data—Measurements specifying the state of the physical environment. Does not include metadata.

Data Inventory—Information about overall data properties for each station within a weather or climate network. A data inventory may include start/stop dates, percentages of available data, breakdowns by climate element, counts of actual data values, counts or fractions of data types, etc. These properties must be determined by actually reading the data and thus require the data to be available, accessible, and in a readable format.

NPS I&M Network—A set of NPS park units grouped by a common theme, typically by natural resource and/or geographic region.

Metadata—Information necessary to interpret environmental data properly, organized as a history or series of snapshots—data about data. Examples include details of measurement processes, station circumstances and exposures, assumptions about the site, network purpose and background, types of observations and sensors, pre-treatment of data, access information, maintenance history and protocols, observational methods, archive locations, owner, and station start/end period.

Quality Assurance—Planned and systematic set of activities to provide adequate confidence that products and services are resulting in credible and correct information. Includes quality control.

Quality Control—Evaluation, assessment, and improvement of imperfect data by utilizing other imperfect data.

Station Inventory—Information about a set of stations obtained from metadata that accompany the network or networks. A station inventory can be compiled from direct and indirect reports prepared by others.

Weather—Instantaneous state of the atmosphere at any given time, mainly with respect to its effects on biological activities. As distinguished from climate, weather consists of the short-term (minutes to days) variations in the atmosphere. Popularly, weather is thought of in terms of temperature, precipitation, humidity, wind, sky condition, visibility, and cloud conditions.

Weather Element (same as Climate Element)—Attribute or property of the state of the atmosphere that is measured, estimated, or derived. Examples of weather elements include temperature, wind speed, wind direction, precipitation amount, precipitation type, relative humidity, dewpoint, solar radiation, snow depth, soil temperature at a given depth, etc. A derived weather element is a function of other elements (like degree days or number of days with rain) and is not measured directly. The terms "parameter" and "variable" are not used to describe weather elements.

Weather Network—Group of weather stations usually owned and maintained by a particular organization and usually for a specific purpose.

Weather Station—Station where collected data are intended for near-real-time use with less need for reference to long-term conditions. In many cases, the detailed circumstances of a set of measurements (siting and exposure, instrument changes, etc.) from weather stations are not as important as for climate stations.

Appendix C. Factors in operating a climate network

C.1. Climate versus Weather
- Climate measurements require _consistency through time._

C.2. Network Purpose
- Anticipated or desired lifetime.
- Breadth of network mission (commitment by needed constituency).
- Dedicated constituency—no network survives without a dedicated constituency.

C.3. Site Identification and Selection
- Spanning gradients in climate or biomes with transects.
- Issues regarding representative spatial scale—site uniformity versus site clustering.
- Alignment with and contribution to network mission.
- Exposure—ability to measure representative quantities.
- Logistics—ability to service station (Always or only in favorable weather?).
- Site redundancy (positive for quality control, negative for extra resources).
- Power—is AC needed?
- Site security—is protection from vandalism needed?
- Permitting often a major impediment and usually underestimated.

C.4. Station Hardware
- Survival—weather is the main cause of lost weather/climate data.
- Robustness of sensors—ability to measure and record in any condition.
- Quality—distrusted records are worthless and a waste of time and money.
  - High quality—will cost up front but pays off later.
  - Low quality—may provide a lower start-up cost but will cost more later (low cost can be expensive).
- Redundancy—backup if sensors malfunction.
- Ice and snow—measurements are much more difficult than rain measurements.
- Severe environments (expense is about two–three times greater than for stations in more benign settings).

C.5. Communications
- Reliability—live data have a much larger constituency.
- One-way or two-way.
  - Retrieval of missed transmissions.
  - Ability to reprogram data logger remotely.
  - Remote troubleshooting abilities.
  - Continuing versus one-time costs.
- Back-up procedures to prevent data loss during communication outages.
- Live communications increase problems but also increase value.

C.6. Maintenance
- Main reason why networks fail (and most networks do eventually fail!).

- <u>Key</u> issue with nearly every network.
- Who will perform maintenance?
- Degree of commitment and motivation to contribute.
- Periodic? On-demand as needed? Preventive?
- Equipment change-out schedules and upgrades for sensors and software.
- Automated stations require <u>skilled</u> and <u>experienced</u> labor.
- Calibration—sensors often drift (climate).
- Site maintenance essential (constant vegetation, surface conditions, nearby influences).
- Typical automated station will cost about $2K per year to maintain.
- Documentation—photos, notes, visits, changes, essential for posterity.
- Planning for equipment life cycle and technological advances.

C.7. Maintaining Programmatic Continuity and Corporate Knowledge
- Long-term vision and commitment needed.
- Institutionalizing versus personalizing—developing appropriate dependencies.

C.8. Data Flow
- Centralized ingest?
- Centralized access to data and data products?
- Local version available?
- Contract out work or do it yourself?
- Quality control of data.
- Archival.
- Metadata—historic information, not a snapshot. Every station should collect metadata.
- Post-collection processing, multiple data-ingestion paths.

C.9. Products
- Most basic product consists of the data values.
- Summaries.
- Write own applications or leverage existing mechanisms?

C.10. Funding
- Prototype approaches as proof of concept.
- Linking and leveraging essential.
- Constituencies—every network <u>needs</u> a constituency.
- Bridging to practical and operational communities? Live data needed.
- Bridging to counterpart research efforts and initiatives—funding source.
- Creativity, resourcefulness, and persistence usually are essential to success.

C.11. Final Comments
- Deployment is by far the easiest part in operating a network.
- Maintenance is the main issue.
- Best analogy: Operating a network is like raising a child; it requires constant attention.

Source: Western Regional Climate Center (WRCC)

Appendix D. Master metadata field list

Field Name	Field Type	Field Description
begin_date	date	Effective beginning date for a record.
begin_date_flag	char(2)	Flag describing the known accuracy of the begin date for a station.
best_elevation	float(4)	Best known elevation for a station (in feet).
clim_div_code	char(2)	Foreign key defining climate division code (primary in table: clim_div).
clim_div_key	int2	Foreign key defining climate division for a station (primary in table: clim_div.
clim_div_name	varchar(30)	English name for a climate division.
controller_info	varchar(50)	Person or organization who maintains the identifier system for a given weather or climate network.
country_key	int2	Foreign key defining country where a station resides (primary in table: none).
county_key	int2	Foreign key defining county where a station resides (primary in table: county).
county_name	varchar(31)	English name for a county.
description	text	Any description pertaining to the particular table.
end_date	date	Last effective date for a record.
end_date_flag	char(2)	Flag describing the known accuracy of station end date.
fips_country_code	char(2)	FIPS (federal information processing standards) country code.
fips_state_abbr	char(2)	FIPS state abbreviation for a station.
fips_state_code	char(2)	FIPS state code for a station.
history_flag	char(2)	Describes temporal significance of an individual record among others from the same station.
id_type_key	int2	Foreign key defining the id_type for a station (usually defined in code).
last_updated	date	Date of last update for a record.
latitude	float(8)	Latitude value.
longitude	float(8)	Longitude value.
name_type_key	int2	"3": COOP station name, "2": best station name.
name	varchar(30)	Station name as known at date of last update entry.
ncdc_state_code	char(2)	NCDC, two-character code identifying U.S. state.
network_code	char(8)	Eight-character abbreviation code identifying a network.
network_key	int2	Foreign key defining the network for a station (primary in table: network).
network_station_id	int4	Identifier for a station in the associated network, which is defined by id_type_key.
remark	varchar(254)	Additional information for a record.
src_quality_code	char(2)	Code describing the data quality for the data source.
state_key	int2	Foreign key defining the U.S. state where a station resides (primary in table: state).
state_name	varchar(30)	English name for a state.
station_alt_name	varchar(30)	Other English names for a station.
station_best_name	varchar(30)	Best, most well-known English name for a station.
time_zone	float4	Time zone where a station resides.
ucan_station_id	int4	Unique station identifier for every station in ACIS.
unit_key	int2	Integer value representing a unit of measure.

Field Name	Field Type	Field Description
updated_by	char(8)	Person who last updated a record.
var_major_id	int2	Defines major climate variable.
var_minor_id	int2	Defines data source within a var_major_id.
zipcode	char(5)	Zipcode where a latitude/longitude point resides.
nps_netcode	char(4)	Network four-character identifier.
nps_netname	varchar(128)	Displayed English name for a network.
parkcode	char(4)	Park four-character identifier.
parkname	varchar(128)	Displayed English name for a park/
im_network	char(4)	NPS I&M network where park belongs (a net code)/
station_id	varchar(16)	Station identifier.
station_id_type	varchar(16)	Type of station identifier.
network.subnetwork.id	varchar(16)	Identifier of a sub-network in associated network.
subnetwork_key	int2	Foreign key defining sub-network for a station.
subnetwork_name	varchar(30)	English name for a sub-network.
slope	integer	Terrain slope at the location.
aspect	integer	Terrain aspect at the station.
gps	char(1)	Indicator of latitude/longitude recorded via GPS (global positioning system).
site_description	text(0)	Physical description of site.
route_directions	text(0)	Driving route or site access directions.
station_photo_id	integer	Unique identifier associating a group of photos to a station. Group of photos all taken on same date.
photo_id	char(30)	Unique identifier for a photo.
photo_date	datetime	Date photograph taken.
photographer	varchar(64)	Name of photographer.
maintenance_date	datetime	Date of station maintenance visit.
contact_key	Integer	Unique identifier associating contact information to a station.
full_name	varchar(64)	Full name of contact person.
organization	varchar(64)	Organization of contact person.
contact_type	varchar(32)	Type of contact person (operator, administrator, etc.)
position_title	varchar(32)	Title of contact person.
address	varchar(32)	Address for contact person.
city	varchar(32)	City for contact person.
state	varchar(2)	State for contact person.
zip_code	char(10)	Zipcode for contact person.
country	varchar(32)	Country for contact person.
email	varchar(64)	E-mail for contact person.
work_phone	varchar(16)	Work phone for contact person.
contact_notes	text(254)	Other details regarding contact person.
equipment_type	char(30)	Sensor measurement type; i.e., wind speed, air temperature, etc.
eq_manufacturer	char(30)	Manufacturer of equipment.
eq_model	char(20)	Model number of equipment.
serial_num	char(20)	Serial number of equipment.
eq_description	varchar(254)	Description of equipment.
install_date	datetime	Installation date of equipment.
remove_date	datetime	Removal date of equipment.
ref_height	integer	Sensor displacement height from surface.
sampling_interval	varchar(10)	Frequency of sensor measurement.

Appendix E. General design considerations for weather/climate-monitoring programs

The process for designing a climate-monitoring program benefits from anticipating design and protocol issues discussed here. Much of this material is been excerpted from a report addressing the Channel Islands National Park (Redmond and McCurdy 2005), where an example is found illustrating how these factors can be applied to a specific setting. Many national park units possess some climate or meteorology feature that sets them apart from more familiar or "standard" settings.

E.1. Introduction

There are several criteria that must be used in deciding to deploy new stations and where these new stations should be sited.

- Where are existing stations located?
- Where have data been gathered in the past (discontinued locations)?
- Where would a new station fill a knowledge gap about basic, long-term climatic averages for an area of interest?
- Where would a new station fill a knowledge gap about how climate behaves over time?
- As a special case for behavior over time, what locations might be expected to show a more sensitive response to climate change?
- How do answers to the preceding questions depend on the climate element? Are answers the same for precipitation, temperature, wind, snowfall, humidity, etc.?
- What role should manual measurements play? How should manual measurements interface with automated measurements?
- Are there special technical or management issues, either present or anticipated in the next 5–15 years, requiring added climate information?
- What unique information is provided in addition to information from existing sites? "Redundancy is bad."
- What nearby information is available to estimate missing observations because observing systems always experience gaps and lose data? "Redundancy is good."
- How would logistics and maintenance affect these decisions?

In relation to the preceding questions, there are several topics that should be considered. The following topics are not listed in a particular order.

E.1.1. Network Purpose

Humans seem to have an almost reflexive need to measure temperature and precipitation, along with other climate elements. These reasons span a broad range from utilitarian to curiosity-driven. Although there are well-known recurrent patterns of need and data use, new uses are always appearing. The number of uses ranges in the thousands. Attempts have been made to categorize such uses (see NRC, 1998; NRC, 2001). Because climate measurements are accumulated over a long time, they should be treated as multi-purpose and should be undertaken in a manner that serves the widest possible applications. Some applications remain constant, while others rise and fall in importance. An insistent issue today may subside, while the next pressing issue of tomorrow barely may be anticipated. The notion that humans might affect the climate of the entire Earth was nearly unimaginable when the national USDA (later NOAA) cooperative weather network began in the late 1800s. Abundant experience has shown, however, that there always will be a demand for a history record of climate measurements and their properties. Experience also shows that there is an expectation that climate measurements will be taken and made available to the general public.

An exhaustive list of uses for data would fill many pages and still be incomplete. In broad terms, however, there are needs to document environmental conditions that disrupt or otherwise affect park operations (e.g., storms and droughts). Design and construction standards are determined by climatological event frequencies that exceed certain thresholds. Climate is a determinant that sometimes attracts and sometimes discourages visitors. Climate may play a large part in the park experience (e.g., Death Valley and heat are nearly synonymous). Some park units are large enough to encompass spatial or elevation diversity in climate, and the sequence of events can vary considerably inside or close to park boundaries. That is, temporal trends and statistics may not be the same everywhere, and this spatial structure should be sampled. The granularity of this structure depends on the presence of topography or large climate gradients or both, such as that found along the U.S. West Coast in summer with the rapid transition from the marine layer to the hot interior.

Plant and animal communities and entire ecosystems react to every nuance in the physical environment. No aspect of weather and climate goes undetected in the natural world. Wilson (1998) proposed "an informal rule of biological evolution" that applies here: "If an organic sensor can be imagined that is capable of detecting any particular environmental signal, a species exists somewhere that possesses this sensor." Every weather and climate event, whether dull or extraordinary to humans, matters to some organism. Dramatic events and creeping incremental change both have consequences to living systems. Extreme events or disturbances can "reset the clock" or "shake up the system" and lead to reverberations that last for years to centuries or longer. Slow change can carry complex nonlinear systems (e.g., any living assemblage) into states where chaotic transitions and new behavior occur. These changes are seldom predictable, typically are observed after the fact, and understood only in retrospect. Climate changes may not be exciting, but as a well-known atmospheric scientist, Mike Wallace, from the University of Washington once noted, "subtle does not mean unimportant".

Thus, individuals who observe the climate should be able to record observations accurately and depict both rapid and slow changes. In particular, an array of artificial influences easily can confound detection of slow changes. The record as provided can contain both real climate variability (that took place in the atmosphere) and fake climate variability (that arose directly from the way atmospheric changes were observed and recorded). As an example, trees growing near a climate station with an excellent anemometer will make it appear that the wind gradually slowed down over many years. Great care must be taken to protect against sources of fake climate variability on the longer-time scales of years to decades. Processes leading to the observed climate are not stationary; rather these processes draw from probability distributions that vary with time. For this reason, climatic time series do not exhibit statistical stationarity. The implications are manifold. There are no true climatic "normals" to which climate inevitably must return. Rather, there are broad ranges of climatic conditions. Climate does not demonstrate exact repetition but instead continual fluctuation and sometimes approximate repetition. In addition, there is always new behavior waiting to occur. Consequently, the business of climate monitoring is never finished, and there is no point where we can state confidently that "enough" is known.

E.1.2. Robustness

The most frequent cause for loss of weather data is the weather itself, the very thing we wish to record. The design of climate and weather observing programs should consider the meteorological equivalent of "peaking power" employed by utilities. Because environmental disturbances have significant effects on ecologic systems, sensors, data loggers, and communications networks should be able to function during the most severe conditions that realistically can be anticipated over the next 50–100 years. Systems designed in this manner are less likely to fail under more ordinary conditions, as well as more likely to transmit continuous, quality data for both tranquil and active periods.

E.1.3. Weather versus Climate

For "weather" measurements, pertaining to what is approximately happening here and now, small moves and changes in exposure are not as critical. For "climate" measurements, where values from different points in time are compared, siting and exposure are critical factors, and it is vitally important that the observing circumstances remain essentially unchanged over the duration of the station record.

Station moves can affect different elements to differing degrees. Even small moves of several meters, especially vertically, can affect temperature records. Hills and knolls act differently from the bottoms of small swales, pockets, or drainage channels (Geiger et al. 2003; Whiteman 2000). Precipitation is probably less subject to change with moves of 50–100 m than other elements (that is, precipitation has less intrinsic variation in small spaces) except if wind flow over the gauge is affected.

E.1.4. Physical Setting

Siting and exposure, and their continuity and consistency through time, significantly influence the climate records produced by a station. These two terms have overlapping connotations. We use the term "siting" in a more general sense, reserving the term "exposure" generally for the particular circumstances affecting the ability of an instrument to record measurements that are representative of the desired spatial or temporal scale.

E.1.5. Measurement Intervals

Climatic processes occur continuously in time, but our measurement systems usually record in discrete chunks of time: for example, seconds, hours, or days. These measurements often are referred to as "systematic" measurements. Interval averages may hide active or interesting periods of highly intense activity. Alternatively, some systems record "events" when a certain threshold of activity is exceeded (examples: another millimeter of precipitation has fallen, another kilometer of wind has moved past, the temperature has changed by a degree, a gust higher than 9.9 m/s has been measured). When this occurs, measurements from all sensors are reported. These measurements are known as "breakpoint" data. In relatively unchanging conditions (long calm periods or rainless weeks, for example), event recorders should send a signal that they are still "alive and well." If systematic recorders are programmed to note and periodically report the highest, lowest, and mean value within each time interval, the likelihood is reduced that interesting behavior will be glossed over or lost. With the capacity of modern data loggers, it is recommended to record and report extremes within the basic time increment (e.g., hourly or 10 minutes). This approach also assists quality-control procedures.

There is usually a trade-off between data volume and time increment, and most automated systems now are set to record approximately hourly. A number of field stations maintained by WRCC are programmed to record in 5- or 10-minute increments, which readily serve to construct an hourly value. However, this approach produces 6–12 times as much data as hourly data. These systems typically do not record details of events at sub-interval time scales, but they easily can record peak values, or counts of threshold exceedance, within the time intervals.

Thus, for each time interval at an automated station, we recommend that several kinds of information—mean or sum, extreme maximum and minimum, and sometimes standard deviation—be recorded. These measurements are useful for quality control and other purposes. Modern data loggers and office computers have quite high capacity. Diagnostic information indicating the state of solar chargers or battery voltages and their extremes is of great value. This topic will be discussed in greater detail in a succeeding section.

Automation also has made possible adaptive or intelligent monitoring techniques where systems vary the recording rate based on detection of the behavior of interest by the software. Sub-interval behavior of interest can be masked on occasion (e.g., a 5-minute extreme downpour with high-erosive capability hidden by an innocuous hourly total). Most users prefer measurements that are systematic in time because they are much easier to summarize and manipulate.

For breakpoint data produced by event reporters, there also is a need to send periodically a signal that the station is still functioning, even though there is nothing more to report. "No report" does not necessarily mean "no data," and it is important to distinguish between the actual observation that was recorded and the content of that observation (e.g., an observation of "0.00" is not the same as "no observation").

E.1.6. Mixed Time Scales
There are times when we may wish to combine information from radically different scales. For example, over the past 100 years we may want to know how the frequency of 5-minute precipitation peaks has varied or how the frequency of peak 1-second wind gusts have varied. We may also want to know over this time if nearby vegetation gradually has grown up to increasingly block the wind or to slowly improve precipitation catch. Answers to these questions require knowledge over a wide range of time scales.

E.1.7. Elements
For manual measurements, the typical elements recorded included temperature extremes, precipitation, and snowfall/snow depth. Automated measurements typically include temperature, precipitation, humidity, wind speed and direction, and solar radiation. An exception to this exists in very windy locations where precipitation is difficult to measure accurately. Automated measurements of snow are improving, but manual measurements are still preferable, as long as shielding is present. Automated measurement of frozen precipitation presents numerous challenges that have not been resolved fully, and the best gauges are quite expensive ($3–8K).

Soil temperatures also are included sometimes. Soil moisture is extremely useful, but measurements are not made at many sites. In addition, care must be taken in the installation and maintenance of instruments used in measuring soil moisture. Soil properties vary tremendously in short distances as well, and it is often very difficult ("impossible") to accurately document these variations (without digging up all the soil!). In cooler climates, ultrasonic sensors that detect snow depth are becoming commonplace.

E.1.8. Wind Standards
Wind varies the most in the shortest distance, since it always decreases to zero near the ground and increases rapidly (approximately logarithmically) with height near the ground. Changes in anemometer height obviously will affect distribution of wind speed as will changes in vegetation, obstructions such as buildings, etc. A site that has a 3-m (10-ft) mast clearly will be less windy than a site that has a 6-m (20-ft) or 10-m (33-ft) mast. Historically, many U.S. airports (FAA and NWS) and most current RAWS sites have used a standard 6-m (20-ft) mast for wind measurements. Some NPS RAWS sites utilize shorter masts. Over the last decade, as Automated Surface Observing Systems (ASOSs, mostly NWS) and Automated Weather Observing Systems (AWOSs, mostly FAA) have been deployed at most airports, wind masts have been raised to 8 or 10 m (26 or 33 ft), depending on airplane clearance. The World Meteorological Organization recommends 10 m as the height for wind measurements (WMO 1983; 2005), and more groups are migrating slowly to this standard. The American Association of State Climatologists (AASC 1985) have recommended that wind be measured at 3 m, a standard geared more for agricultural applications than for general purpose uses where higher levels usually are preferred. Different anemometers have different starting thresholds; therefore, areas that frequently experience very light winds may not produce wind measurements thus affecting long-term mean estimates of wind speed. For both sustained winds (averages over a short interval of 2–60 minutes) and especially for gusts, the duration of the sampling interval makes a considerable difference. For the same wind history, 1–second gusts are higher than gusts averaging 3 seconds, which in turn are greater than 5-second averages, so that the same sequence would be described with different numbers (all three systems and more are in use). Changes in the averaging procedure, or in height or exposure, can lead to "false" or "fake" climate change with no change in actual climate. Changes in any of these should be noted in the metadata.

E.1.9. Wind Nomenclature
Wind is a vector quantity having a direction and a speed. Directions can be two- or three-dimensional; they will be three-dimensional if the vertical component is important. In all common uses, winds always are denoted by the direction they blow *from* (north wind or southerly breeze). This convention exists because wind often brings weather, and thus our attention is focused upstream. However, this approach contrasts with the way ocean currents are viewed. Ocean currents usually are denoted by the direction they are moving *towards* (eastward current moves from west to east). In specialized applications (such as in atmospheric modeling), wind velocity vectors point in the direction that the wind is blowing. Thus, a southwesterly wind (from the southwest) has both northward and eastward (to the north and to the east) components. Except near mountains, wind cannot blow up or down near the ground, so the vertical component of wind often is approximated as zero, and the horizontal component is emphasized.

E.1.10. Frozen Precipitation

Frozen precipitation is more difficult to measure than liquid precipitation, especially with automated techniques. Goodison et al. (1998), Sevruk and Harmon (1984), Yang et al. (1998, 2001) provide many of the reasons to explain this. The importance of frozen precipitation varies greatly from one setting to another. This subject was discussed in greater detail in a related inventory and monitoring report for the Alaska park units (Redmond et al. 2005).

In climates that receive frozen precipitation, a decision must be made whether or not to try to record such events accurately. This usually means that the precipitation must be turned into liquid either by falling into an antifreeze fluid solution that is then weighed or by heating the precipitation enough to melt and fall through a measuring mechanism such as a nearly-balanced tipping bucket. Accurate measurements from the first approach require expensive gauges; tipping buckets can achieve this resolution readily but are more apt to lose some or all precipitation. Improvements have been made to the heating mechanism on the NWS tipping-bucket gauge used for the ASOS to correct its numerous deficiencies making it less problematic; however, this gauge is not inexpensive. A heat supply needed to melt frozen precipitation usually requires more energy than renewable energy (solar panels or wind recharging) can provide thus AC power is needed. The availability of AC power is severely limited in many cold or remote U. S. settings. Furthermore, periods of frozen precipitation or rime often provide less-than-optimal recharging conditions with heavy clouds, short days, low-solar-elevation angles and more horizon blocking, and cold temperatures causing additional drain on the battery.

E.1.11. Save or Lose

A second consideration with precipitation is determining if the measurement should be saved (as in weighing systems) or lost (as in tipping-bucket systems). With tipping buckets, after the water has passed through the tipping mechanism, it usually just drops to the ground. Thus, there is no checksum to ensure that the sum of all the tips adds up to what has been saved in a reservoir at some location. By contrast, the weighing gauges continually accumulate until the reservoir is emptied, the reported value is the total reservoir content (for example, the height of the liquid column in a tube), and the incremental precipitation is the difference in depth between two known times. These weighing gauges do not always have the same fine resolution. Some gauges only record to the nearest centimeter, which is usually acceptable for hydrology but not necessarily for other needs. (For reference, a millimeter of precipitation can get a person in street clothes quite wet.) This is how the NRCS/USDA SNOTEL system works in climates that measure up to 3000 cm of snow in a winter. (See http://www.wcc.nrcs.usda.gov/publications for publications or http://www.wcc.nrcs.usda.gov/factpub/aib536.html for a specific description.) No precipitation is lost this way. A thin layer of oil is used to suppress evaporation, and anti-freeze ensures that frozen precipitation melts. When initially recharged, the sum of the oil and starting antifreeze solution is treated as the zero point. The anti-freeze usually is not sufficiently environmentally friendly to discharge to the ground and thus must be hauled into the area and then back out. Other weighing gauges are capable of measuring to the 0.25-mm (0.01-in.) resolution but do not have as much capacity and must be emptied more often. Day/night and storm-related thermal expansion and contraction and sometimes wind shaking can cause fluid pressure from accumulated totals to go up and down in SNOTEL gauges by small increments (commonly 0.3-3 cm, or 0.01–0.10 ft) leading to "negative precipitation" followed by similarly non-real light precipitation when, in fact, no change took place in the amount of accumulated precipitation.

E.1.12. Time

Time should always be in local standard time (LST), and daylight savings time (DST) should never be used under any circumstances with automated equipment and timers. Using DST leads to one duplicate hour, one missing hour, and a season of displaced values, as well as needless confusion and a data-management nightmare. Absolute time, such as Greenwich Mean Time (GMT) or Coordinated Universal Time (UTC), also can be used because these formats are unambiguously translatable. Since measurements only provide information about what already *has* occurred or *is* occurring and not what *will* occur, they should always be assigned to the *ending time* of the associated interval with hour 24 marking the end of the last hour of the day. In this system, midnight always represents the end of the day, not the start. To demonstrate the importance of this differentiation, we have encountered situations where police officers seeking corroborating weather data could not recall whether the time on their crime report from a year ago was the starting midnight or the ending midnight! Station positions should be known to within a few meters, easily accomplished with GPS, so that time zones and solar angles can be determined accurately.

E.1.13. Automated versus Manual

Most of this report has addressed automated measurements. Historically, most measurements are manual and typically collected once a day. In many cases, manual measurements continue because of habit, usefulness, and desire for continuity over time. Manual measurements are extremely useful and when possible should be encouraged. However, automated measurements are becoming more common. For either, it is important to record time in a logically consistent manner.

It should not be automatically assumed that newer data and measurements are "better" than older data or that manual data are "worse" than automated data. Older or simpler manual measurements are often of very high quality even if they sometimes are not in the most convenient digital format.

There is widespread desire to use automated systems to reduce human involvement. This is admirable and understandable, but every automated weather/climate station or network requires significant human attention and maintenance. A telling example concerns the Oklahoma Mesonet (see Brock et al. 1995, and bibliography at http://www.mesonet.ou.edu), a network of about 115 high–quality, automated meteorological stations spread over Oklahoma, where about 80 percent of the annual ($2–3M) budget is nonetheless allocated to humans with only about 20 percent allocated to equipment.

E.1.14. Manual Conventions

Manual measurements typically are made once a day. Elements usually consist of maximum and minimum temperature, temperature at observation time, precipitation, snowfall, snow depth, and sometimes evaporation, wind, or other information. Since it is not actually known when extremes occurred, the only logical approach, and the nationwide convention, is to ascribe the entire measurement to the time-interval date and to enter it on the form in that way. For morning observers (for example, 8 am to 8 am), this means that the maximum temperature written for today often is from yesterday afternoon and sometimes the minimum temperature for the 24-hr period actually occurred yesterday morning. However, this is understood and expected. It is often a surprise to observers to see how many maximum temperatures do not occur in the afternoon and how many minimum temperatures do not occur in the predawn hours. This is especially true in environments that are colder, higher, northerly, cloudy, mountainous, or coastal. As long as this convention is strictly followed every day, it has been shown that truly excellent climate records can result (Redmond 1992). Manual observers should reset equipment only one time per day at the official observing time. Making more than one measurement a day is discouraged strongly; this practice results in a hybrid record that is too difficult to interpret. The only exception is for total daily snowfall. New snowfall can be measured up to four times per day with no observations closer than six hours. It is well known that more frequent measurement of snow increases the annual total because compaction is a continuous process.

Two main purposes for climate observations are to establish the long-term averages for given locations and to track variations in climate. Broadly speaking, these purposes address topics of absolute and relative climate behavior. Once absolute behavior has been "established" (a task that is never finished because long-term averages continue to vary in time)—temporal variability quickly becomes the item of most interest.

E.2. Representativeness

Having discussed important factors to consider when new sites are installed, we now turn our attention to site "representativeness." In popular usage, we often encounter the notion that a site is "representative" of another site if it receives the same annual precipitation or records the same annual temperature or if some other element-specific, long-term average has a similar value. This notion of representativeness has a certain limited validity, but there are other aspects of this idea that need to be considered.

A climate monitoring site also can be said to be representative if climate records from that site show sufficiently strong temporal correlations with a large number of locations over a sufficiently large area. If station A receives 20 cm a year and station B receives 200 cm a year, these climates obviously receive quite differing amounts of precipitation. However, if their monthly, seasonal, or annual correlations are high (for example, 0.80 or higher for a particular time scale), one site can be used as a surrogate for estimating values at the other if measurements for a particular month, season, or year are missing. That is, a wet or dry month at one station is also a wet or dry month (relative to its own mean) at the comparison station. Note that high correlations on one time scale do not imply automatically that high correlations will occur on other time scales.

Likewise, two stations having similar mean climates (for example, similar annual precipitation) might not co-vary in close synchrony (for example, coastal versus interior). This may be considered a matter of climate "affiliation" for a particular location.

Thus, the representativeness of a site can refer either to the basic climatic averages for a given duration (or time window within the annual cycle) or to the extent that the site co-varies in time with respect to all surrounding locations. One site can be representative of another in the first sense but not the second, or vice versa, or neither, or both—all combinations are possible. If two sites are perfectly correlated then, in a sense, they are "redundant." However, redundancy has value because all sites will experience missing data especially with automated equipment in rugged environments and harsh climates where outages and other problems nearly can be guaranteed. In many cases, those outages are caused by the weather, particularly by unusual weather and the very conditions we most wish to know about. Methods for filling in those values will require proxy information from this or other nearby networks. Thus, redundancy is a virtue rather than a vice.

In general, the cooperative stations managed by the NWS have produced much longer records than automated stations like RAWS or SNOTEL stations. The RAWS stations often have problems with precipitation, especially in winter, or with missing data, so that low correlations may be data problems rather than climatic dissimilarity. The RAWS records also are relatively short, so correlations should be interpreted with care. In performing and interpreting such analyses, however, we must remember that there are physical climate reasons and observational reasons why stations within a short distance (even a few tens or hundreds of meters) may not correlate well.

E.2.1. Temporal Behavior

It is possible that high correlations will occur between station pairs during certain portions of the year (i.e., January) but low correlations may occur during other portions of the year (e.g., September or October). The relative contributions of these seasons to the annual total (for precipitation) or average (for temperature) and the correlations for each month are both factors in the correlation of an aggregated time window of longer duration that encompasses those seasons (e.g., one of the year definitions such as calendar year or water year). A complete and careful evaluation ideally would include such a correlation analysis but requires more resources and data. Note that it also is possible and frequently is observed that temperatures are highly correlated while precipitation is not or vice versa, and these relations can change according to the time of year. If two stations are well correlated for all climate elements for all portions of the year, then they can be considered redundant.

With scarce resources, the initial strategy should be to try to identify locations that do not correlate particularly well, so that each new site measures something new that cannot be guessed easily from the behavior of surrounding sites. (An important caveat here is that lack of such correlation could be a result of physical climate behavior and not a result of faults with the actual measuring process; i.e., by unrepresentative or simply poor-quality data. Unfortunately, we seldom have perfect climate data.) As additional sites are added, we usually wish for some combination of unique and redundant sites to meet what amounts to essentially orthogonal constraints: new information and more reliably-furnished information.

A common consideration is whether to observe on a ridge or in a valley, given the resources to place a single station within a particular area of a few square kilometers. Ridge and valley stations will correlate very well for temperatures when lapse conditions prevail, particularly summer daytime temperatures. In summer at night or winter at daylight, the picture will be more mixed and correlations will be lower. In winter at night when inversions are common and even the rule, correlations may be zero or even negative and perhaps even more divergent as the two sites are on opposite sides of the inversion. If we had the luxury of locating stations everywhere, we would find that ridge tops generally correlate very well with other ridge tops and similarly valleys with other valleys, but ridge tops correlate well with valleys only under certain circumstances. Beyond this, valleys and ridges having similar orientations usually will correlate better with each other than those with perpendicular orientations, depending on their orientation with respect to large-scale wind flow and solar angles.

Unfortunately, we do not have stations everywhere, so we are forced to use the few comparisons that we have and include a large dose of intelligent reasoning, using what we have observed elsewhere. In performing and interpreting such analyses, we must remember that there are physical climatic reasons and observational reasons why stations within a short distance (even a few tens or hundreds of meters) may not correlate well.

Examples of correlation analyses include those for the Channel Islands and for southwest Alaska, which can be found in Redmond and McCurdy (2005) and Redmond et al. (2005). These examples illustrate what can be learned from correlation analyses. Spatial correlations generally vary by time of year. Thus, results should be displayed in the form of annual correlation cycles—for monthly mean temperature and monthly total precipitation and perhaps other climate elements like wind or humidity—between station pairs selected for climatic setting and data availability and quality.

In general, the COOP stations managed by the NWS have produced much longer records than have automated stations like RAWS or SNOTEL stations. The RAWS stations also often have problems with precipitation, especially in winter or with missing data, so that low correlations may be data problems rather than climate dissimilarity. The RAWS records are much shorter, so correlations should be interpreted with care, but these stations are more likely to be in places of interest for remote or under-sampled regions.

E.2.2. Spatial Behavior

A number of techniques exist to interpolate from isolated point values to a spatial domain. For example, a common technique is simple inverse distance weighting. Critical to the success of the simplest of such techniques is that some other property of the spatial domain, one that is influential for the mapped element, does not vary significantly. Topography greatly influences precipitation, temperature, wind, humidity, and most other meteorological elements. Thus, this criterion clearly is not met in any region having extreme topographic diversity. In such circumstances, simple Cartesian distance may have little to do with how rapidly correlation deteriorates from one site to the next, and in fact, the correlations can decrease readily from a mountain to a valley and then increase again on the next mountain. Such structure in the fields of spatial correlation is not seen in the relatively (statistically) well-behaved flat areas like those in the eastern United States.

To account for dominating effects such as topography and inland–coastal differences that exist in certain regions, some kind of additional knowledge must be brought to bear to produce meaningful, physically plausible, and observationally based interpolations. Historically, this has proven to be an extremely difficult problem, especially to perform objective and repeatable analyses. An analysis performed for southwest Alaska (Redmond et al. 2005) concluded that the PRISM (Parameter Regression on Independent Slopes Model) maps (Daly et al. 1994, 2002; Gibson et al., 2002; Doggett et al., 2004) were probably the best available. An analysis by Simpson et al. (2005) further discussed many issues in the mapping of Alaska's climate and resulted in the same conclusion about PRISM.

E.2.3. Climate-Change Detection

Although general purpose climate stations should be situated to address all aspects of climate variability, it is desirable that they also be in locations that are more sensitive to climate change from natural or anthropogenic influences should it begin to occur. The question here is how well we know such sensitivities. The polar regions and especially the North Pole are generally regarded as being more sensitive to changes in radiative forcing of climate because of positive feedbacks. The climate-change issue is quite complex because it encompasses more than just greenhouse gasses.

Sites that are in locations or climates particularly vulnerable to climate change should be favored. How this vulnerability is determined is a considerably challenging research issue. Candidate locations or situations are those that lie on the border between two major biomes or just inside the edge of one or the other. In these cases, a slight movement of the boundary in anticipated direction (toward "warmer," for example) would be much easier to detect as the boundary moves past the site and a different set of biota begin to be established. Such a vegetative or ecologic response would be more visible and would take less time to establish as a real change than would a smaller change in the center of the distribution range of a marker or key species.

E.2.4. Element-Specific Differences

The various climate elements (temperature, precipitation, cloudiness, snowfall, humidity, wind speed and direction, solar radiation) do not vary through time in the same sequence or manner nor should they necessarily be expected to vary in this manner. The spatial patterns of variability should not be expected to be the same for all elements. These patterns also should not be expected to be similar for all months or seasons. The suitability of individual sites for measurement also varies from one element to another. A site that has a favorable exposure for temperature or wind may not have a favorable exposure for precipitation or snowfall. A site that experiences proper air movement may be situated in a topographic channel, such as a river valley or a pass, which restricts the range of wind directions and affects the distribution of speed-direction categories.

E.2.5. Logistics and Practical Factors

Even with the most advanced scientific rationale, sites in some remote or climatically challenging settings may not be suitable because of the difficulty in servicing and maintaining equipment. Contributing to these challenges are scheduling difficulties, animal behavior, snow burial, icing, snow behavior, access and logistical problems, and the weather itself. Remote and elevated sites usually require far more attention and expense than a rain-dominated, easily accessible valley location.

For climate purposes, station exposure and the local environment should be maintained in their original state (vegetation especially), so that changes seen are the result of regional climate variations and not of trees growing up, bushes crowding a site, surface albedo changing, fire clearing, etc. Repeat photography has shown many examples of slow environmental change in the vicinity of a station in rather short time frames (5–20 years), and this technique should be employed routinely and frequently at all locations. In the end, logistics, maintenance, and other practical factors almost always determine the success of weather- and climate-monitoring activities.

E.2.6. Personnel Factors

Many past experiences (almost exclusively negative) strongly support the necessity to place primary responsibility for station deployment and maintenance in the hands of seasoned, highly qualified, trained, and meticulously careful personnel, the more experienced the better. Over time, even in "benign" climates but especially where harsher conditions prevail, every conceivable problem will occur and both the usual and unusual should be anticipated: weather, animals, plants, salt, sensor and communication failure, windblown debris, corrosion, power failures, vibrations, avalanches, snow loading and creep, corruption of the data logger program, etc. An ability to anticipate and forestall such problems, a knack for innovation and improvisation, knowledge of electronics, practical and organizational skills, and presence of mind to bring the various small but vital parts, spares, tools, and diagnostic troubleshooting equipment are highly valued qualities. Especially when logistics are so expensive, a premium should be placed on using experienced personnel, since the slightest and seemingly most minor mistake can render a station useless or, even worse, uncertain. Exclusive reliance on individuals without this background can be costly and almost always will result eventually in unnecessary loss of data. Skilled labor and an apprenticeship system to develop new skilled labor will greatly reduce (but not eliminate) the types of problems that can occur in operating a climate network.

E.3. Site Selection

In addition to considerations identified previously in this appendix, various factors need to be considered in selecting sites for new or augmented instrumentation.

E.3.1. Equipment and Exposure Factors

E.3.1.1. Measurement Suite: All sites should measure temperature, humidity, wind, solar radiation, and snow depth. Precipitation measurements are more difficult but probably should be attempted with the understanding that winter measurements may be of limited or no value unless an all-weather gauge has been installed. Even if an all-weather gauge has been installed, it is desirable to have a second gauge present that operates on a different principle–for example, a fluid-based system like those used in the SNOTEL stations in tandem with a higher–resolution, tipping bucket gauge for summertime. Without heating, a tipping bucket gauge usually is of use only when temperatures are above freezing and when temperatures have not been below freezing for some time, so that accumulated ice and snow is not melting and being recorded as present precipitation. Gauge undercatch is a significant issue in snowy climates, so shielding should be considered for all gauges designed to work over the winter months. It is very important to note the presence or absence of shielding, the type of shielding, and the dates of installation or removal of the shielding.

E.3.1.2. Overall Exposure: The ideal, general all-purpose site has gentle slopes, is open to the sun and the wind, has a natural vegetative cover, avoids strong local (less than 200 m) influences, and represents a reasonable compromise among all climate elements. The best temperature sites are not the best precipitation sites, and the same is true for other elements. Steep topography in the immediate vicinity should be avoided unless settings where precipitation is affected by steep topography are being deliberately sought or a mountaintop or ridgeline is the desired location. The potential for disturbance should be considered: fire and flood risk, earth movement, wind-borne debris, volcanic deposits or lahars, vandalism, animal tampering, and general human encroachment are all factors.

E.3.1.3. Elevation: Mountain climates do not vary in time in exactly the same manner as adjoining valley climates. This concept is emphasized when temperature inversions are present to a greater degree and during precipitation when winds rise up the slopes at the same angle. There is considerable concern that mountain climates will be (or already are) changing and perhaps changing differently than lowland climates, which has direct and indirect consequences for plant and animal life in the more extreme zones. Elevations of special significance are those that are near the mean rain/snow line for winter, near the tree line, and near the mean annual freezing level (all of these may not be quite the same). Because the lapse rates in wet climates often are nearly moist-adiabatic during the main precipitation seasons, measurements at one elevation may be extrapolated to nearby elevations. In drier climates and in the winter, temperature and to a lesser extent wind will show various elevation profiles.

E.3.1.4. Transects: The concept of observing transects that span climatic gradients is sound. This is not always straightforward in topographically uneven terrain, but these transects could still be arranged by setting up station(s) along the coast; in or near passes atop the main coastal interior drainage divide; and inland at one, two, or three distances into the interior lowlands. Transects need not—and by dint of topographic constraints probably cannot—be straight lines, but the closer that a line can be approximated the better. The main point is to systematically sample the key points of a behavioral transition without deviating too radically from linearity.

E.3.1.5. Other Topographic Considerations: There are various considerations with respect to local topography. Local topography can influence wind (channeling, upslope/downslope, etc.), precipitation (orographic enhancement, downslope evaporation, catch efficiency, etc.), and temperature (frost pockets, hilltops, aspect, mixing or decoupling from the overlying atmosphere, bowls, radiative effects, etc.), to different degrees at differing scales. In general, for measurements to be areally representative, it is better to avoid these local effects to the extent that they can be identified before station deployment (once deployed, it is desirable not to move a station). The primary purpose of a climate-monitoring network should be to serve as an infrastructure in the form of a set of benchmark stations for comparing other stations. Sometimes, however, it is exactly these local phenomena that we want to capture. Living organisms, especially plants, are affected by their immediate environment, whether it is representative of a larger setting or not. Specific measurements of limited scope and duration made for these purposes then can be tied to the main benchmarks. This experience is useful also in determining the complexity needed in the benchmark monitoring process in order to capture particular phenomena at particular space and time scales.

Sites that drain (cold air) well generally are better than sites that allow cold air to pool. Slightly sloped areas (1 degree is fine) or small benches from tens to hundreds of meters above streams are often favorable locations. Furthermore, these sites often tend to be out of the path of hazards (like floods) and to have rocky outcroppings where controlling vegetation will not be a major concern. Benches or wide spots on the rise between two forks of a river system are often the only flat areas and sometimes jut out to give greater exposure to winds from more directions.

E.3.1.6. Prior History: The starting point in designing a program is to determine what kinds of observations have been collected over time, by whom, in what manner, and if these observation are continuing to the present time. It also may be of value to "re-occupy" the former site of a station that is now inactive to provide some measure of continuity or a reference point from the past. This can be of value even if continuous observations were not made during the entire intervening period.

E.3.2. Element-Specific Factors

E.3.2.1. Temperature: An open exposure with uninhibited air movement is the preferred setting. The most common measurement is made at approximately eye level, 1.5–2.0 m. In snowy locations sensors should be at least one meter higher than the deepest snowpack expected in the next 50 years or perhaps 2–3 times the depth of the average maximum annual depth. Sensors should be shielded above and below from solar radiation (bouncing off snow), from sunrise/sunset horizontal input, and from vertical rock faces. Sensors should be clamped tightly, so that they do not swivel away from level stacks of radiation plates. Nearby vegetation should be kept away from the sensors (several meters). Growing vegetation should be cut to original conditions. Small hollows and swales can cool tremendously at night, and it is best avoid these areas. Side slopes of perhaps a degree or two of angle facilitate air movement and drainage and, in effect, sample a large area during nighttime hours. The very bottom of a valley should be avoided. Temperature can change substantially from moves of only a few meters. Situations have been observed where flat and seemingly uniform conditions (like airport runways) appear to demonstrate different climate behaviors over short distances of a few tens or hundreds of meters (differences of 5–10°C). When snow is on the ground, these microclimatic differences can be stronger, and differences of 2–5°C can occur in the short distance between the thermometer and the snow surface on calm evenings.

E.3.2.2. Precipitation (liquid): Calm locations with vegetative or artificial shielding are preferred. Wind will adversely impact readings; therefore, the less the better. Wind effects on precipitation are far less for rain than for snow. Devices that "save" precipitation present advantages, but most gauges are built to dump precipitation as it falls or to empty periodically. Automated gauges give both the amount and the timing. Simple backups that record only the total precipitation since the last visit have a certain advantage (for example, storage gauges or lengths of PVC pipe perhaps with bladders on the bottom). The following question should be asked: Does the total precipitation from an automated gauge add up to the measured total in a simple bucket (evaporation is prevented with an appropriate substance such as mineral oil)? Drip from overhanging foliage and trees can augment precipitation totals.

E.3.2.3. Precipitation (frozen): Calm locations or shielding are a must. Undercatch for rain is only about 5 percent, but with winds of only 2–4 m/s, gauges may catch only 30–70 percent of the actual snow falling depending on density of the flakes. To catch 100 percent of the snow, the standard configuration for shielding is employed by the CRN (Climate Reference Network): the DFIR (Double-Fence Intercomparison Reference) shield with 2.4-m (8-ft.) vertical, wooden slatted fences in two concentric octagons with diameters of 8 m and 4 m (26 ft and 13 ft, respectively) and an inner Alter shield (flapping vanes). Numerous tests have shown this is the only way to achieve complete catch of snowfall (e.g., Yang et al. 1998, 2001). The DFIR shield is large and bulky; it is recommended that all precipitation gauges have at least Alter shields on them.

Near the coast, much snow is heavy and falls more vertically. In colder locations or storms, light flakes frequently will fly in and then out of the gauge. Clearings in forests are usually excellent sites. Snow blowing from trees that are too close can augment actual precipitation totals. Artificial shielding (vanes, etc.) placed around gauges in snowy locales always should be used if accurate totals are desired. Moving parts tend to freeze up. Capping of gauges during heavy snowfall events is a common occurrence. When the cap becomes pointed, snow falls off to the ground and is not recorded. Caps and plugs often will not fall into the tube until hours, days, or even weeks have passed, typically during an extended period of freezing temperature or above or when sunlight finally occurs. Liquid-based measurements (e.g., SNOTEL "rocket" gauges) do not have the resolution (usually 0.3 cm [0.1 in.] rather than 0.03 cm [0.01 in.]) that tipping bucket and other gauges have but are known to be reasonably accurate in very snowy climates. Light snowfall events might not be recorded until enough of them add up to the next reporting increment. More expensive gauges like Geonors can be considered and could do quite well in snowy settings; however, they need to be emptied every 40 cm (15 in.) or so (capacity of 51 cm [20 in.]) until the new 91-cm (36-in.) capacity gauge is offered for sale. Recently, the NWS has been trying out the new (and very expensive) Ott all-weather gauge. Riming can be an issue in windy foggy environments below freezing. Rime, dew, and other forms of atmospheric condensation are not real precipitation, since they are caused by the gauge.

E.3.2.4. Snow Depth: Windswept areas tend to be blown clear of snow. Conversely, certain types of vegetation can act as a snow fence and cause artificial drifts. However, some amount of vegetation in the vicinity generally can help slow down the wind. The two most common types of snow-depth gauges are the Judd Snow Depth Sensor, produced by Judd Communications, and the snow depth gauge produced by Campbell Scientific, Inc. Opinions vary on which one is better. These gauges use ultrasound and look downward in a cone about 22 degrees in diameter. The ground should be relatively clear of vegetation and maintained in a manner so that the zero point on the calibration scale does not change.

E.3.2.5. Snow Water Equivalent: This is determined by the weight of snow on fluid-filled pads about the size of a desktop set up sometimes in groups of four or in larger hexagons several meters in diameter. These pads require flat ground some distance from nearby sources of windblown snow and shielding that is "just right": not too close to the shielding to act as a kind of snow fence and not too far from the shielding so that blowing and drifting become a factor. Generally, these pads require fluids that possess antifreeze-like properties, as well as handling and replacement protocols.

E.3.2.6. Wind: Open exposures are needed for wind measurements. Small prominences or benches without blockage from certain sectors are preferred. A typical rule for trees is to site stations back 10 tree-heights from all tree obstructions. Sites in long, narrow valleys can obviously only exhibit two main wind directions. Gently rounded eminences are more favored. Any kind of topographic steering should be avoided to the extent possible. Avoiding major mountain chains or single isolated mountains or ridges is usually a favorable approach, if there is a choice. Sustained wind speed and the highest gusts (1-second) should be recorded. Averaging methodologies for both sustained winds and gusts can affect climate trends and should be recorded as metadata with all changes noted. Vegetation growth affects the vertical wind profile, and growth over a few years can lead to changes in mean wind speed even if the "real" wind does not change, so vegetation near the site (perhaps out to 50 m) should be maintained in a quasi-permanent status (same height and spatial distribution). Wind devices can rime up and freeze or spin out of balance. In severely rimed or windy climates, rugged anemometers, such as those made by Taylor, are worth considering. These anemometers are expensive but durable and can withstand substantial abuse. In exposed locations, personnel should plan for winds to be at least 50 m/s and be able to measure these wind speeds. At a minimum, anemometers should be rated to 75 m/s.

E.3.2.7. Humidity: Humidity is a relatively straightforward climate element. Close proximity to lakes or other water features can affect readings. Humidity readings typically are less accurate near 100 percent and at low humidities in cold weather.

E.3.2.8. Solar Radiation: A site with an unobstructed horizon obviously is the most desirable. This generally implies a flat plateau or summit. However, in most locations trees or mountains will obstruct the sun for part of the day.

E.3.2.9. Soil Temperature: It is desirable to measure soil temperature at locations where soil is present. If soil temperature is recorded at only a single depth, the most preferred depth is 10 cm. Other common depths include 25 cm, 50 cm, 2 cm, and 100 cm. Biological activity in the soil will be proportional to temperature with important threshold effects occurring near freezing.

E.3.2.10. Soil Moisture: Soil-moisture gauges are somewhat temperamental and require care to install. The soil should be characterized by a soil expert during installation of the gauge. The readings may require a certain level of experience to interpret correctly. If accurate, readings of soil moisture are especially useful.

E.3.2.11. Distributed Observations: It can be seen readily that compromises must be struck among the considerations described in the preceding paragraphs because some are mutually exclusive.

How large can a "site" be? Generally, the equipment footprint should be kept as small as practical with all components placed next to each other (within less than 10–20 m or so). Readings from one instrument frequently are used to aid in interpreting readings from the remaining instruments.

What is a tolerable degree of separation? Some consideration may be given to locating a precipitation gauge or snow pillow among protective vegetation, while the associated temperature, wind, and humidity readings would be collected more effectively in an open and exposed location within 20–50 m. Ideally, it is advantageous to know the wind measurement precisely at the precipitation gauge, but a compromise involving a short split, and in effect a "distributed observation," could be considered. There are no definitive rules governing this decision, but it is suggested that the site footprint be kept within approximately 50 m. There also are constraints imposed by engineering and electrical factors that affect cable lengths, signal strength, and line noise; therefore, the shorter the cable the better. Practical issues include the need to trench a channel to outlying instruments or to allow lines to lie atop the ground and associated problems with animals, humans, weathering, etc. Separating a precipitation gauge up to 100 m or so from an instrument mast may be an acceptable compromise if other factors are not limiting.

E.3.2.12. Instrument Replacement Schedules: Instruments slowly degrade, and a plan for replacing them with new, refurbished, or recalibrated instruments should be in place. After approximately five years, a systematic change-out procedure should result in replacing most sensors in a network. Certain parts, such as solar radiation sensors, are candidates for annual calibration or change-out. Anemometers tend to degrade as bearings erode or electrical contacts become uneven. Noisy bearings are an indication, and a stethoscope might aid in hearing such noises. Increased internal friction affects the threshold starting speed; once spinning, they tend to function properly. Increases in starting threshold speeds can lead to more zero-wind measurements and thus reduce the reported mean wind speed with no real change in wind properties. A field calibration kit should be developed and taken on all site visits, routine or otherwise. Rain gauges can be tested with drip testers during field visits. Protective conduit and tight water seals can prevent abrasion and moisture problems with the equipment, although seals can keep moisture in as well as out. Bulletproof casings sometimes are employed in remote settings. A supply of spare parts, at least one of each and more for less-expensive or more-delicate sensors, should be maintained to allow replacement of worn or nonfunctional instruments during field visits. In addition, this approach allows instruments to be calibrated in the relative convenience of the operational home—the larger the network, the greater the need for a parts depot.

E.3.3. Long-Term Comparability and Consistency

E.3.3.1. Consistency: The emphasis here is to hold biases constant. Every site has biases, problems, and idiosyncrasies of one sort or another. The best rule to follow is simply to try to keep biases constant through time. Since the goal is to track climate through time, keeping sensors, methodologies, and exposure constant will ensure that only true climate change is being measured. This means leaving the site in its original state or performing maintenance to keep it that way. Once a site is installed, the goal should be to never move the site even by a few meters or to allow significant changes to occur within 100 m for the next several decades.

Sites in or near rock outcroppings likely will experience less vegetative disturbance or growth through the years and will not usually retain moisture, a factor that could speed corrosion. Sites that will remain locally similar for some time are usually preferable. However, in some cases the intent of a station might be to record the local climate effects of changes within a small-scale system (for example, glacier, recently burned area, or scene of some other disturbance) that is subject to a regional climate influence. In this example, the local changes might be much larger than the regional changes.

E.3.3.2. Metadata: Since the climate of every site is affected by features in the immediate vicinity, it is vital to record this information over time and to update the record repeatedly at each service visit. Distances, angles, heights of vegetation, fine-scale topography, condition of instruments, shielding discoloration, and other factors from within a meter to several kilometers should be noted. Systematic photography should be undertaken and updated at least once every one–two years.

Photographic documentation should be taken at each site in a standard manner and repeated every two–three years. Guidelines for methodology were developed by Redmond (2004) as a result of experience with the NOAA CRN and can be found on the WRCC NPS Web pages at http://www.wrcc.dri.edu/nps and at ftp://ftp.wrcc.dri.edu/nps/photodocumentation.pdf.

The main purpose for climate stations is to *track climatic conditions through time*. Anything that affects the interpretation of records through time must to be noted and recorded for posterity. The important factors should be clear to a person who has never visited the site, no matter how long ago the site was installed.

In regions with significant, climatic transition zones, transects are an efficient way to span several climates and make use of available resources. Discussions on this topic at greater detail can be found in Redmond and Simeral (2004) and in Redmond et al. (2005).

E.4. Literature Cited

American Association of State Climatologists. 1985. Heights and exposure standards for sensors on automated weather stations. The State Climatologist **9**.

Brock, F. V., K. C. Crawford, R. L. Elliott, G. W. Cuperus, S. J. Stadler, H. L. Johnson and M. D. Eilts. 1995. The Oklahoma Mesonet: A technical overview. Journal of Atmospheric and Oceanic Technology **12**:5-19.

Daly, C., R. P. Neilson, and D. L. Phillips. 1994. A statistical-topographic model for mapping climatological precipitation over mountainous terrain. Journal of Applied Meteorology **33**:140-158.

Daly, C., W. P. Gibson, G. H. Taylor, G. L. Johnson, and P. Pasteris. 2002. A knowledge-based approach to the statistical mapping of climate. Climate Research **22**:99-113.

Doggett, M., C. Daly, J. Smith, W. Gibson, G. Taylor, G. Johnson, and P. Pasteris. 2004. High-resolution 1971-2000 mean monthly temperature maps for the western United States. Fourteenth AMS Conf. on Applied Climatology, 84th AMS Annual Meeting. Seattle, WA, American Meteorological Society, Boston, MA, January 2004, Paper 4.3, CD-ROM.

Geiger, R., R. H. Aron, and P. E. Todhunter. 2003. The Climate Near the Ground. 6th edition. Rowman & Littlefield Publishers, Inc., New York.

Gibson, W. P., C. Daly, T. Kittel, D. Nychka, C. Johns, N. Rosenbloom, A. McNab, and G. Taylor. 2002. Development of a 103-year high-resolution climate data set for the conterminous United States. Thirteenth AMS Conf. on Applied Climatology. Portland, OR, American Meteorological Society, Boston, MA, May 2002:181-183.

Goodison, B. E., P. Y. T. Louie, and D. Yang. 1998. WMO solid precipitation measurement intercomparison final report. WMO TD 982, World Meteorological Organization, Geneva, Switzerland.

National Research Council. 1998. Future of the National Weather Service Cooperative Weather Network. National Academies Press, Washington, D.C.

National Research Council. 2001. A Climate Services Vision: First Steps Toward the Future. National Academies Press, Washington, D.C.

Redmond, K. T. 1992. Effects of observation time on interpretation of climatic time series - A need for consistency. Eighth Annual Pacific Climate (PACLIM) Workshop. Pacific Grove, CA, March 1991:141-150.

Redmond, K. T. 2004. Photographic documentation of long-term climate stations. Available from ftp://ftp.wrcc.dri.edu/nps/photodocumentation.pdf. (accessed 15 August 2004)

Redmond, K. T. and D. B. Simeral. 2004. Climate monitoring comments: Central Alaska Network Inventory and Monitoring Program. Available from ftp://ftp.wrcc.dri.edu/nps/alaska/cakn/npscakncomments040406.pdf. (accessed 6 April 2004)

Redmond, K. T., D. B. Simeral, and G. D. McCurdy. 2005. Climate monitoring for southwest Alaska national parks: network design and site selection. Report 05-01. Western Regional Climate Center, Reno, Nevada.

Redmond, K. T., and G. D. McCurdy. 2005. Channel Islands National Park: Design considerations for weather and climate monitoring. Report 05-02. Western Regional Climate Center, Reno, Nevada.

Sevruk, B., and W. R. Hamon. 1984. International comparison of national precipitation gauges with a reference pit gauge. Instruments and Observing Methods, Report No 17, WMO/TD – 38, World Meteorological Organization, Geneva, Switzerland.

Simpson, J. J., Hufford, G. L., C. Daly, J. S. Berg, and M. D. Fleming. 2005. Comparing maps of mean monthly surface temperature and precipitation for Alaska and adjacent areas of Canada produced by two different methods. Arctic **58**:137-161.

Whiteman, C. D. 2000. Mountain Meteorology: Fundamentals and Applications. Oxford

University Press, Oxford, UK.

Wilson, E. O. 1998. Consilience: The Unity of Knowledge. Knopf, New York.

World Meteorological Organization. 1983. Guide to meteorological instruments and methods of observation, No. 8, 5th edition, World Meteorological Organization, Geneva Switzerland.

World Meteorological Organization. 2005. Organization and planning of intercomparisons of rainfall intensity gauges. World Meteorological Organization, Geneva Switzerland.

Yang, D., B. E. Goodison, J. R. Metcalfe, V. S. Golubev, R. Bates, T. Pangburn, and C. Hanson. 1998. Accuracy of NWS 8" standard nonrecording precipitation gauge: results and application of WMO intercomparison. Journal of Atmospheric and Oceanic Technology **15**:54-68.

Yang, D., B. E. Goodison, J. R. Metcalfe, P. Louie, E. Elomaa, C. Hanson, V. Bolubev, T. Gunther, J. Milkovic, and M. Lapin. 2001. Compatibility evaluation of national precipitation gauge measurements. Journal of Geophysical Research **106**:1481-1491.

Appendix F. Descriptions of weather/climate monitoring networks

F.1. Pacific Northwest Cooperative Agricultural Network (AgriMet)
- Purpose of network: provide weather/climate data for regional crop water use modeling, frost monitoring, and various agricultural research projects in the Pacific Northwest.
- Primary management agency: BLM.
- Data website: http://www.usbr.gov/pn/agrimet/wxdata.html.
- Measured weather/climate elements:
  o Air temperature.
  o Relative humidity and dewpoint temperature.
  o Precipitation.
  o Wind speed.
  o Solar radiation.
- Sampling frequency: hourly.
- Reporting frequency: hourly; some stations report every 10 minutes if real-time communications are available.
- Estimated station cost: $12K with maintenance costs around $2K/year.
- Network strengths:
  o AgriMet has near-real-time data.
  o Period of record is relatively long.
  o Sites are well maintained.
- Network weaknesses:
  o Only agricultural sites are sampled.
  o AgriMet has a limited geographic extent (Pacific Northwest).

AgriMet is a satellite-based network of automated weather stations operated by the BLM. Stations in AgriMet are located primarily in irrigated agricultural areas throughout the Pacific Northwest.

F.2. NOAA Air Resources Laboratory Field Research Division (ARL FRD)
- Purpose of network: improve understanding of atmospheric transport, atmospheric dispersion, and air-surface exchange processes.
- Primary management agency: NOAA.
- Data website: http://www.noaa.inl.gov/.
- Measured weather/climate elements:
  o Air temperature.
  o Precipitation.
  o Relative humidity.
  o Wind speed.
  o Wind direction.
  o Wind gust.
  o Gust direction.
  o Solar radiation.
- Sampling frequency: unknown.

- Reporting frequency: five minutes.
- Estimated station cost: varies from $10K to $40K, depending on instrumentation.
- Network strengths:
  o High-quality data.
  o Sites are well maintained.
- Network weaknesses:
  o Density of station coverage is localized, concentrated in specific study areas.

The mission of the ARL FRD is to improve understanding of atmospheric transport, atmospheric dispersion, and air-surface exchange processes. The ARL FRD operates various mesonets in support of tracer studies and other meteorological research. Some of these mesonets include the San Joaquin Valley Air Quality Study, the Central California Ozone Study, and the Utah County Carbon Monoxide Study. In the UCBN, The ARL FRD has supported the Department of Energy's Idaho National Laboratory since the late 1940s by providing meteorological forecasts and emergency response capabilities. Meteorological observations at these sites generally include temperature, precipitation, humidity, wind, and solar radiation. Other measurements conducted at ARL FRD stations include evaporation, transpiration, and near-surface trace gas fluxes.

F.3. Canadian weather/climate stations (CANADA)
- Purpose of network: provide weather/climate data for forecasting and climate-monitoring efforts in Canada.
- Primary management agency: The Meteorological Service of Canada.
- Data website: http://www.weatheroffice.ec.gc.ca/canada_e.html.
- Measured weather/climate elements:
  o Air temperature.
  o Barometric pressure.
  o Relative humidity and dewpoint temperature.
  o Precipitation.
  o Wind speed and direction.
  o Wind gust and direction.
  o Solar radiation.
  o Sky Cover.
  o Ceiling.
  o Visibility.
- Sampling frequency: hourly.
- Reporting frequency: hourly.
- Estimated station cost: unknown.
- Network strengths:
  o Data are of high quality.
  o Periods of record are relatively long.
  o Sites are well maintained.
- Network weaknesses:
  o Sites are only in Canada, so usefulness limited to northern NPS park units.
  o Limited data access.

These include various automated weather/climate station networks from Canada. The Meteorological Service of Canada operates many of these stations, including airport sites. The data measured at these sites generally include temperature, precipitation, humidity, wind, pressure, sky cover, ceiling, visibility, and current weather. Most of the data records are of high quality.

F.4. NWS Cooperative Observer Program (COOP)

- Purpose of network:
  - o Provide observational, meteorological data required to define U.S. climate and help measure long-term climate changes.
  - o Provide observational, meteorological data in near real-time to support forecasting and warning mechanisms and other public service programs of the NWS.
- Primary management agency: NOAA (NWS).
- Data websites: data are available from the NCDC (http://www.ncdc.noaa.gov), RCCs (e.g., WRCC, http://www.wrcc.dri.edu), and state climate offices.
- Measured weather/climate elements
  - o Maximum, minimum, and observation-time temperature.
  - o Precipitation, snowfall, snow depth.
  - o Pan evaporation (some stations).
- Sampling frequency: daily.
- Reporting frequency: daily or monthly (station-dependent).
- Estimated station cost: $2K with maintenance costs of $500–900/year.
- Network strengths:
  - o Decade–century records at most sites.
  - o Widespread national coverage (thousands of stations).
  - o Excellent data quality when well maintained.
  - o Relatively inexpensive; highly cost effective.
  - o Manual measurements; not automated.
- Network weaknesses:
  - o Uneven exposures; many are not well-maintained.
  - o Dependence on schedules for volunteer observers.
  - o Slow entry of data from many stations into national archives.
  - o Data subject to observational methodology; not always documented.
  - o Manual measurements; not automated and not hourly.

The COOP network has long served as the main climate observation network in the United States. Readings are usually made by volunteers using equipment supplied, installed, and maintained by the federal government. The observer in effect acts as a host for the data-gathering activities and supplies the labor; this is truly a "cooperative" effort. The SAO sites often are considered to be part of the cooperative network as well if they collect the previously mentioned types of weather/climate observations. Typical observation days are morning to morning, evening to evening, or midnight to midnight. By convention, observations are ascribed to the date the instrument was reset at the end of the observational period. For this reason, midnight observations represent the end of a day. The Historical Climate Network is a subset of the cooperative network but contains longer and more complete records.

F.5. Citizen Weather Observer Program (CWOP)

- Purpose of network: collect observations from private citizens and make these data available for homeland security and other weather applications, providing constant feedback to the observers to maintain high data quality.
- Primary management agency: NOAA MADIS program.
- Data website: http://www.wxqa.com.
- Measured weather/climate elements:
  - o Air temperature.
  - o Dewpoint temperature.
  - o Precipitation.
  - o Wind speed and direction.
  - o Barometric pressure.
- Sampling frequency: 15 minutes or less.
- Reporting frequency: 15 minutes.
- Estimated station cost: unknown.
- Network strengths:
  - o Active partnership between public agencies and private citizens.
  - o Large number of participant sites.
  - o Regular communications between data providers and users, encouraging higher data quality.
- Network weaknesses:
  - o Variable instrumentation platforms.
  - o Metadata are sometimes limited.

The CWOP network is a public-private partnership with U.S. citizens and various agencies including NOAA, NASA (National Aeronautics and Space Administration), and various universities. There are over 4500 registered sites worldwide, with close to 3000 of these sites located in North America.

F.6. NPS Gaseous Pollutant Monitoring Program (GPMP)

- Purpose of network: measurement of ozone and related meteorological elements.
- Primary management agency: NPS.
- Data website: http://www2.nature.nps.gov/air/monitoring.
- Measured weather/climate elements:
  - o Air temperature.
  - o Relative humidity.
  - o Precipitation.
  - o Wind speed and direction.
  - o Solar radiation.
  - o Surface wetness.
- Sampling frequency: continuous.
- Reporting frequency: hourly.
- Estimated station cost: unknown.
- Network strengths:
  - o Stations are located within NPS park units.

o Data quality is excellent, with high data standards.

o Provides unique measurements that are not available elsewhere.

o Records are up to 2 decades in length.

o Site maintenance is excellent.

o Thermometers are aspirated.

- Network weaknesses:

o Not easy to download the entire data set or to ingest live data.

o Period of record is short compared to other automated networks. Earliest sites date from 2004.

o Station spacing and coverage: station installation is episodic, driven by opportunistic situations.

The NPS web site indicates that there are 33 sites with continuous ozone analysis run by NPS, with records from a few to about 16-17 years. Of these stations, 12 are labeled as GPMP sites and the rest are labeled as Clean Air Status and Trends Network (CASTNet) sites. All of these have standard meteorological measurements, including a 10-m mast. Another nine GPMP sites are located within NPS units but run by cooperating agencies. A number of other sites (1-2 dozen) ran for differing periods in the past, generally less than 5-10 years.

F.7. Idaho Transportation Department Network (ITD)

- Purpose of network: provide weather data to support management of Idaho's transportation network.
- Primary management agency: ITD.
- Data websites: http://itd.idaho.gov and http://www.met.utah.edu/jhorel/html/mesonet.
- Measured weather/climate elements:

o Air temperature.

o Relative humidity.

o Pressure.

o Wind speed and direction.

o Wind gust and direction.

- Sampling frequency: unknown.
- Reporting frequency: unknown.
- Estimated station cost: unknown.
- Network strengths:

o Real-time data.

- Network weaknesses:

o Coverage is limited to the state of Idaho.

o Access to archived data is difficult.

These weather stations are operated by ITD in support of management activities for Idaho's transportation network. Measured meteorological elements include temperature, precipitation, wind, and relative humidity.

F.8. KBCI TV, Boise, Idaho (KBCI)

- Purpose of network: provide near-real-time meteorological data to KBCI in support of KBCI's daily weather segments on their daily news programs.

- Primary management agency: KBCI TV.
- Data website: http://www.met.utah.edu/jhorel/html/mesonet.
- Measured weather/climate elements:
  o Air temperature.
  o Relative humidity.
  o Precipitation.
  o Wind speed and direction.
  o Wind gust and direction.
- Sampling frequency: unknown.
- Reporting frequency: unknown.
- Estimated station cost: unknown.
- Network strengths:
  o Real-time data.
- Network weaknesses:
  o Uncertain data quality and station maintenance.
  o Coverage limited to southern Idaho.
  o No access to archived data.

Weather stations in this network are operated by volunteers supported by KBCI TV in Boise, Idaho. These stations provide near-real-time data to KBCI in support of KBCI's daily weather segments on their daily news programs. Measured meteorological elements include temperature, precipitation, wind, and relative humidity.

F.9. Montana Counties Soil Climate Network (MCSCN)
- Purpose of network: provide near-real-time meteorological data to support drought monitoring efforts in the state of Montana.
- Primary management agency: Montana Natural Resource Information System.
- Data websites: http://nris.state.mt.us/drought/ and http://www.met.utah.edu/jhorel/html/mesonet.
- Measured weather/climate elements:
  o Air temperature.
  o Precipitation.
  o Wind speed and direction.
  o Wind gust and direction.
- Sampling frequency: unknown.
- Reporting frequency: unknown.
- Estimated station cost: unknown.
- Network strengths:
  o Real-time data.
- Network weaknesses:
  o Uncertain data quality and station maintenance.
  o Network started very recently, so no long-term climate records.

This network was initiated in response to the need to monitor drought conditions in the state of Montana. This network provides near-real-time information on rainfall and soil moisture, along with any other data that is useful for drought assistance. Soil moisture and temperature measurements are taken at depths of 6, 12, 18, and 30 inches (15, 30, 46, and 76 cm). Measured meteorological elements include temperature, precipitation, wind speed and direction.

F.10. NWS Forecast Office, Missoula, Montana (MSOWFO)
- Purpose of network: provide near-real-time local meteorological data to assist in routine weather forecast development for western Montana.
- Primary management agency: NWS forecast office, Missoula, Montana.
- Data website: http://www.met.utah.edu/jhorel/html/mesonet.
- Measured weather/climate elements:
  o Air temperature.
  o Relative humidity.
  o Precipitation.
  o Wind speed and direction.
  o Wind gust and direction.
- Sampling frequency: unknown.
- Reporting frequency: unknown.
- Estimated station cost: unknown.
- Network strengths:
  o Real-time data.
- Network weaknesses:
  o Uncertain data quality and station maintenance.
  o Coverage limited to western Montana.

These are near-real-time stations managed by the NWS forecast office in Missoula, Montana. Data from these stations are used to provide local weather data to assist in developing routine weather forecasts for western Montana. Measured meteorological elements include temperature, precipitation, wind, and relative humidity.

F.11. Oregon Department of Transportation Network (ODOT)
- Purpose of network: provide weather data to support management of Oregon's transportation network.
- Primary management agency: ODOT.
- Data websites: http://www.oregon.gov/ODOT and http://www.met.utah.edu/jhorel/html/mesonet.
- Measured weather/climate elements:
  o Air temperature.
  o Relative humidity.
  o Pressure.
  o Wind speed and direction.
  o Wind gust and direction.
- Sampling frequency: unknown.
- Reporting frequency: unknown.
- Estimated station cost: unknown.
- Network strengths:

o Real-time data.
o Routine station maintenance.
- Network weaknesses:
  o Coverage is limited to the state of Oregon.
  o Access to archived data can be difficult.

These weather stations are operated by ODOT in support of management activities for Oregon's transportation network. Measured meteorological elements include temperature, precipitation, wind, and relative humidity.

F.12. NWS Forecast Office, Pendleton, Oregon (PDTWFO)
- Purpose of network: provide near-real-time local meteorological data to assist in routine weather forecast development for central and eastern Oregon.
- Primary management agency: NWS forecast office, Pendleton, Oregon.
- Data website: http://www.met.utah.edu/jhorel/html/mesonet.
- Measured weather/climate elements:
  o Air temperature.
  o Relative humidity.
  o Precipitation.
  o Wind speed and direction.
  o Wind gust and direction.
- Sampling frequency: unknown.
- Reporting frequency: unknown.
- Estimated station cost: unknown.
- Network strengths:
  o Real-time data.
- Network weaknesses:
  o Uncertain data quality and station maintenance.
  o Coverage limited to central and eastern Oregon.

These are near-real-time stations managed by the NWS forecast office in Pendleton, Oregon. Data from these stations are used to provide local weather data to assist in developing routine weather forecasts for central and eastern Oregon. Measured meteorological elements include temperature, precipitation, wind, and relative humidity.

F.13. Remote Automated Weather Station Network (RAWS)
- Purpose of network: provide near-real-time (hourly or near hourly) measurements of meteorological variables for use in fire weather forecasts and climatology. Data from RAWS also are used for natural resource management, flood forecasting, natural hazard management, and air-quality monitoring.
- Primary management agency: WRCC, National Interagency Fire Center.
- Data website: http://www.raws.dri.edu/index.html.
- Measured weather/climate elements:
  o Air temperature.
  o Precipitation.
  o Relative humidity.

- o Wind speed.
- o Wind direction.
- o Wind gust.
- o Gust direction.
- o Solar radiation.
- o Soil moisture and temperature.
- Sampling frequency: 1 or 10 minutes, element-dependent.
- Reporting frequency: generally hourly. Some stations report every 15 or 30 minutes.
- Estimated station cost: $12K with satellite telemetry ($8K without satellite telemetry); maintenance costs are around $2K/year.
- Network strengths:
  - o Metadata records are usually complete.
  - o Sites are located in remote areas.
  - o Sites are generally well-maintained.
  - o Entire period of record available on-line.
- Network weaknesses:
  - o RAWS network is focused largely on fire management needs (formerly focused only on fire needs).
  - o Frozen precipitation is not measured reliably.
  - o Station operation is not always continuous.
  - o Data transmission is completed via one-way telemetry. Data are therefore recoverable either in real-time or not at all.

The RAWS network is used by many land-management agencies, such as the BLM, NPS, Fish and Wildlife Service, Bureau of Indian Affairs, Forest Service, and other agencies. The RAWS network was one of the first automated weather station networks to be installed in the United States. Most gauges do not have heaters, so hydrologic measurements are of little value when temperatures dip below freezing or reach freezing after frozen precipitation events. There are approximately 1,100 real-time sites in this network and about 1,800 historic sites (some are decommissioned or moved). The sites can transmit data all winter but may be in deep snow in some locations. The WRCC is the archive for this network and receives station data and metadata through a special connection to the National Interagency Fire Center in Boise, Idaho.

F.14. NWS/FAA Surface Airways Observation Network (SAO)
- Purpose of network: provide near-real-time (hourly or near hourly) measurements of meteorological variables and are used both for airport operations and weather forecasting.
- Primary management agency: NOAA, FAA.
- Data websites: data are available from state climate offices, RCCs (e.g., WRCC, http://www.wrcc.dri.edu), and NCDC (http://www.ncdc.noaa.gov).
- Measured weather/climate elements:
  - o Air temperature.
  - o Dewpoint and/or relative humidity.
  - o Wind speed.
  - o Wind direction.
  - o Wind gust.
  - o Gust direction.

- o Barometric pressure.
- o Precipitation (not at many FAA sites).
- o Sky cover.
- o Ceiling (cloud height).
- o Visibility.
- Sampling frequency: element-dependent.
- Reporting frequency: element-dependent.
- Estimated station cost: $100–$200K with maintenance costs approximately $10K/year.
- Network strengths:
  - o Records generally extend over several decades.
  - o Consistent maintenance and station operations.
  - o Data record is reasonably complete and usually high quality.
  - o Hourly or sub-hourly data.
- Network weaknesses:
  - o Nearly all sites are located at airports.
  - o Data quality can be related to size of airport—smaller airports tend to have poorer datasets.
  - o Influences from urbanization and other land-use changes.

These stations are managed by NOAA, U. S. Navy, U. S. Air Force, and FAA. These stations are located generally at major airports and military bases. The FAA stations often do not record precipitation, or they may provide precipitation records of reduced quality. Automated stations are typically ASOSs for the NWS or AWOSs for the FAA. Some sites only report episodically with observers paid per observation.

F.15. USDA/NRCS Snowfall Telemetry (SNOTEL) Network

- Purpose of network: collect snowpack and related climate data to assist in forecasting water supply in the western United States.
- Primary management agency: NRCS.
- Data website: http://www.wcc.nrcs.usda.gov/snow/.
- Measured weather/climate elements:
  - o Air temperature.
  - o Precipitation.
  - o Snow water content.
  - o Snow depth.
  - o Relative humidity (enhanced sites only).
  - o Wind speed (enhanced sites only).
  - o Wind direction (enhanced sites only).
  - o Solar radiation (enhanced sites only).
  - o Soil moisture and temperature (enhanced sites only).
- Sampling frequency: 1-minute temperature; 1-hour precipitation, snow water content, and snow depth. Less than one minute for relative humidity, wind speed and direction, solar radiation, and soil moisture and temperature (all at enhanced site configurations only).
- Reporting frequency: reporting intervals are user-selectable. Commonly used intervals are every one, two, three, or six hours.
- Estimated station cost: $20K with maintenance costs approximately $2K/year.

- Network strengths:
  o Sites are located in high-altitude areas that typically do not have other weather or climate stations.
  o Data are of high quality and are largely complete.
  o Very reliable automated system.
- Network weaknesses:
  o Historically limited number of elements.
  o Remote so data gaps can be long.
  o Metadata sparse and not high quality; site histories are lacking.
  o Measurement and reporting frequencies vary.
  o Many hundreds of mountain ranges still not sampled.
  o Earliest stations were installed in the late 1970s; temperatures have only been recorded since the 1980s.

USDA/NRCS maintains a set of automated snow-monitoring stations known as the SNOTEL (snowfall telemetry) network. These stations are designed specifically for cold and snowy locations. Precipitation and snow water content measurements are intended for hydrologic applications and water-supply forecasting, so these measurements are measured generally to within 2.5 mm (0.1 in.). Snow depth is tracked to the nearest 25 mm, or one inch (25 mm). These stations function year around.

F.16. USDA/NRCS Snowcourse Network (NRCS-SC)
- Purpose of network: collect snowpack and related climate data to assist in forecasting water supply in the western United States.
- Primary management agency: NRCS.
- Data website: http://www.wcc.nrcs.usda.gov/snowcourse/.
- Measured weather/climate elements:
  o Snow depth.
  o Snow water equivalent.
- Measurement, reporting frequency: monthly or seasonally.
- Estimated station cost: cost of man-hours needed to set up snowcourse and make measurements.
- Network strengths
  o Periods of record are generally long.
  o Large number of high-altitude sites.
- Network weaknesses
  o Measurement and reporting only occurs on monthly to seasonal basis.
  o Few weather/climate elements are measured.

USDA/NRCS maintains another network of snow-monitoring stations in addition to SNOTEL. These sites are known as snowcourses. Many of these sites have been in operation since the early part of the twentieth century. These are all manual sites where only snow depth and snow water content are measured.

F.17. Union Pacific Railroad Network (UPR)

- Purpose of network: provide near-real-time meteorological data to support the shipping and transport activities of the Union Pacific Railroad.
- Primary management agency: Union Pacific Railroad.
- Data website: http://www.met.utah.edu/jhorel/html/mesonet.
- Measured weather/climate elements:
  o Air temperature.
  o Relative humidity.
  o Precipitation.
  o Wind speed and direction.
  o Wind gust and direction.
- Sampling frequency: unknown.
- Reporting frequency: unknown.
- Estimated station cost: unknown.
- Network strengths:
  o Real-time data.
  o Fairly extensive network (covers much of central and western U.S.)
- Network weaknesses:
  o Uncertain data quality and station maintenance.
  o Access to archived data is difficult.

This is a network of weather stations managed by UPR to support their shipping and transport activities, primarily in the central and western U.S. These stations are generally located along the UPR's main railroad lines. Measured meteorological elements include temperature, precipitation, wind, and relative humidity.

F.18. Washington State Department of Transportation Network (WA DOT)

- Purpose of network: provide weather data to support management of the state of Washington's transportation network.
- Primary management agency: Washington State Department of Transportation.
- Data websites: http://www.wsdot.wa.gov and http://www.met.utah.edu/jhorel/html/mesonet.
- Measured weather/climate elements:
  o Air temperature.
  o Relative humidity.
  o Precipitation.
  o Wind speed and direction.
  o Wind gust and direction.
- Sampling frequency: unknown.
- Reporting frequency: unknown.
- Estimated station cost: unknown.
- Network strengths:
  o Real-time data.
- Network weaknesses:
  o Coverage is limited to the state of Washington.

o Access to archived data is difficult.

These weather stations are operated by the Washington State Department of Transportation in support of management activities for the state of Washington's transportation network. Measured meteorological elements include temperature, precipitation, wind, and relative humidity.

Appendix G. Electronic supplements

G.1. ACIS metadata file for weather and climate stations associated with the UCBN: http://www.wrcc.dri.edu/nps/pub/UCBN/metadata/UCBN_from_ACIS.tar.gz.

NPS/UCBN/NRTR—2006/012, November 2006